BASIC TECHNIQUES ◆ ADVANCED RESULTS

FROM

FineScale MODELER MAGAZINE

LE MODELING HANDBOOK NO. 15

HOW TO BUILD
SCALE MODELS

Straight from the box
JAY ZVOLANEK

Seams like a breeze
LANCE NORMAN

Masking and attaching canopies
CHRISTOPHER BOWIE

Building your first tank kit
TERRY SUNDAY

Modeling a NASCAR Winston Cup winner
BILL COULTER

Building your first waterline ship kit
DENNIS MOORE

Structures and groundwork for your first diorama
JACK SMITH

The art of stretching sprue
BOB DYE and MICHAEL MACKOWSKI

Realistic light lenses for models
JIM STEEL

Details make the difference
RAY SORENSON

Ten ways to improve your 1/24 scale NASCAR racer model
TIM BONGARD

Basics of detailing armor models
HAL SANFORD

Battle damage for armored vehicles
HAL SANFORD

52 **Modeling stowed equipment on military vehicles**
HAL SANFORD

55 **Detailing aircraft cockpits**
BOB STEINBRUNN

60 **Installing photoetched cockpit details**
BOB STEINBRUNN

66 **Detailing small-scale ship models**
CRAIG SCOGIN

71 **Photoetching for modelers**
PAUL BUDZIK

74 **Modeling slings, straps, and buckles**
HILBER H. GRAF

76 **Airbrushing tips from the experts**

81 **Painting German tank camouflage**
TONY GREENLAND

85 **An easy way to paint road wheels**
ROBERT SKURDA

86 **Painting natural-metal finishes**
LARRY SCHRAMM

90 **Drawing aircraft panel lines with pencil**
RUSTY WHITE

92 **Painting faces in artist's oils**
GEORGE DeWOLFE

97 **Simulating wood planking with tape**
RUSTY WHITE

98 **The delights (and disasters) of decaling**
PAUL BOYER

104 **Sources**

Editor: Mark Hembree
Art Director: Lawrence Luser
Artists: Glenda Wiesendanger, Lisa Bergman, Phil Kirchmeier
FSM Staff Photographers: Chris Becker, Art Schmidt, Darla Gawelski
Cover photos: Bob Steinbrunn, 1/48 scale Spitfire Mk. IX; Tony Greenland, 1/35 scale Tiger I.

KALMBACH BOOKS

Jay's 1/48 scale Testor P-51D Mustang was the first airplane model he built since he got back into the hobby after high school and college. Built out of the box and with a minimum of tools and materials, he proves you don't have to be a master modeler to build a decent-looking model.

STEP BY STEP

Straight from the box

Building your first plastic airplane

BY JAY ZVOLANEK

W E'RE GOING TO do something that most veteran FSM readers may find unusual — this article is aimed at modelers who are attracted to the high-quality models they see in the magazine, but say "I could never do that." There's hope! You can build a clean, good-looking model with only the stuff that comes out of the carton, a few tools, paint, and small amounts of skill and patience.

I used to build plastic airplanes when I was a kid back in the sixties, but quit while I was in college. I started up again in the mid-seventies, but built mostly wood and metal model railroad kits. Recently, I decided it would be fun to try something different — a plastic airplane kit — and to see what I could do without getting carried away.

What you need. Many of the items

you'll need to build a plastic kit can be found around the house, Fig. 1. Cut a grocery bag open to use as a cover for your table or workbench. Its plain brown color will help you see tiny parts, too. Grab a few clear plastic sandwich bags to hold small parts and subassemblies. They can also be used to mask large portions of the model when painting. Tweezers are a must for holding small parts. Toothpicks can be used for stirring paint and straight pins are helpful for applying cement. Disposable bottle caps are ideal containers for dabs of cement and small amounts of paint.

Scotch tape, clothespins, and rubber bands are all useful for holding parts together as the glue dries — be careful that cement doesn't creep under them and ruin your model. White glue is good for attaching delicate parts and for filling tiny gaps. I wipe my models

with alcohol-soaked cotton swabs be fore painting to eliminate oily finge prints that might repel paint. I use la quer thinner to clean brushes ar airbrush parts; a quart will last a lor time. Finally, a roll of paper towels great for cleaning up.

A trip to the hobby shop. Sele something simple for your first a tempt — this is supposed to be an er joyable hobby, so don't dive in too dee right away. I bought a Testor 1/48 sca ($\frac{1}{4}'' = 1'$) P-51D Mustang (No. 587). was big enough so that I could see wha I was doing, had an interesting col scheme, and wasn't too complex.

Figure 2 shows some of the bas items you'll need to buy at the hobb shop. Buy both liquid and tube-typ plastic cements. The liquid type is a plied with a brush and sets quickly; th tube type is thicker and easier to us Also buy a tube of putty for fillin seams and pits. You'll need a smal fine-toothed, half-round file and 320 400-grit sandpaper or fine sanding fil for cleaning up and while you're at buy a hobby knife and replacemer blades. You can use single-edge razo blades for some cutting, but for fir work you'll need the control these littl scalpels provide. The blades wear ou fast, so replace them often.

Paints. Even though many kits ar molded in the color of the actual ai plane, your model should be painte Once you've assured the person behin the counter that you really are going t buy a particular kit, he should let yo

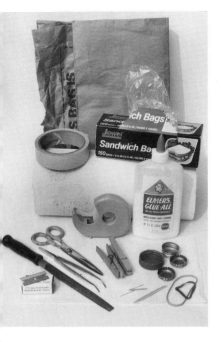

Fig. 1. Not everything you need to build models is found in the hobby shop. Paper bags, paper towels, rubber bands, tape, and tools can probably be found around the house.

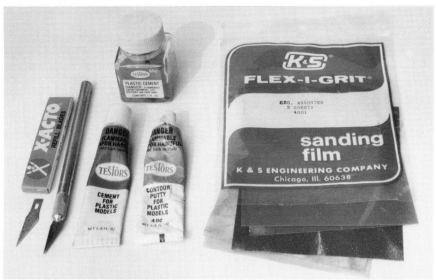

Fig. 2. A good hobby knife is essential — get extra blades, too. Buy both liquid and tube cements. Filler putty and sandpaper make those seams disappear.

open the box to figure out what colors of paint you'll need. Usually, he'll also give you advice as to the best paints to use, Fig. 3.

Brushes are the time-honored tool for painting models, and until recently, they were the only way I painted. Buy three brushes: a 1/4" flat for large areas, a medium (1/8") round for all-around paint and cement application, and a fine (00 or smaller) round for touch-up and details.

Spray cans are another choice. They can lay on a uniform coat of paint without leaving brush marks. However, they have a wide spray pattern and are the most expensive way to paint. You can get around the first problem by careful masking. Buy three cans: medium gray for use as a primer, clear gloss, and clear flat for oversprays.

Airbrushes are easier to control than spray cans and don't leave brush marks. Properly thinned, regular model paints can be sprayed through an airbrush — and they're more economical than spray cans. On the other hand, airbrushes can be difficult to work with and maintain, they need a source of compressed air, and good-quality airbrushes are not cheap.

You don't have to invest hundreds of dollars on an airbrush and compressor. I use a simple Badger 250 and propellant cans, Fig. 4, a setup that costs about $30. This model has a 2" spray diameter, giving more control than a spray can. An airbrush is cheaper to use than spray cans and you can choose from a wider variety of colors. The only

Fig. 3. A wide variety of model paints and brushes is available. Spray cans of primer, clear gloss, and clear flat should be in your paint collection. A bottle of decal-setting solution will make decals snuggle down over the model's surface detail.

recurring expense is the propellant cans. A big one will do about six to ten 1/48 scale fighters.

One final item to buy is decal-setting solution. If softens decals and allows them to snuggle down tight against the model's surface.

A place to work. Once you've rushed home with your treasures, stop for a second and consider where you're going to assemble this masterpiece. Building any model takes time; cement has to

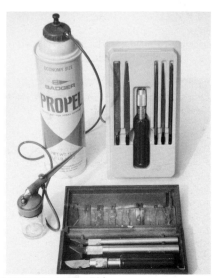

Fig. 4. An inexpensive airbrush with a propellant can (left) allows you to spray a large assortment of bottled paints. Files (top right) let you shape or remove excess plastic and putty faster than sandpaper. Knife sets (bottom) come in handy when you make modifications to kits.

set and paint needs to dry — most models aren't one-evening projects. I spent about 12 hours spread over 7 sessions in 3 weeks building and finishing this Mustang. Fortunately, I have about 2 square feet of my basement workbench to dedicate to modeling.

When I lived in a small apartment, I kept my tools in one cigar box, my paints in another, and the kit in its box. I stored them in the closet between modeling sessions. Take a look around. You want to be able to relax and enjoy yourself with this project, but be considerate of the rest of the household, too.

Take precautions to keep your work area and yourself from being sprayed along with your model. First, work in a well-ventilated area, like a workshop with a window vent fan. I rigged one up using a standard bathroom blower hooked up to a dryer vent. While you're at it, protect your lungs with a pollen mask from the drugstore. These won't stop the smell, but they will help you avoid inhaling floating paint particles.

Make a disposable spray booth from a cardboard carton lined with grocery bags. Set it up on a level surface and keep your light at least four feet away to prevent it from being a fire hazard. Cover your hand with a plastic bag while you hold the model. Also, be careful when you take the cap off the can — I managed to shoot myself with a spray can during this project. Some fast work with thinner and spray cleaner saved my shirt, but I had trouble explaining to my wife how I acquired a silver belly button. Wearing an apron is a good idea.

Wait! Not yet. Before you start modeling, sit down and read the kit instructions. These range from a simple exploded-view diagram to an eight-page booklet like the one in the Mustang kit. Some are poorly written and some are in foreign languages, so make sure you understand each step before you jump in and come out gluing. See if all the parts are there and in good shape. For example, my kit's canopy was cracked, so I wrote to Testor describing the problem and included the kit and part numbers. I received a replacement by return mail.

A

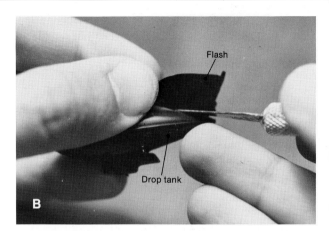

Flash

Drop tank

B

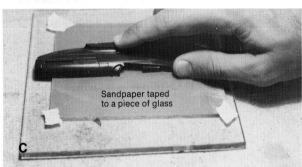

Sandpaper taped to a piece of glass

C

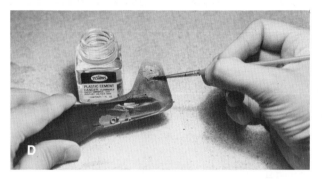

D

Step 1. Assembly. To avoid confusion and to prevent loss of small parts, leave them on the sprues (the plastic trees or runners that hold the parts) until you need them. Also, it's easier to paint small parts while they're still attached to the sprues. When you need a small part, place the sprue in a plastic food storage bag and cut the parts off with a razor blade or hobby knife, **A**. Occasionally you'll run into flash — thin excess plastic that forms when the molten plastic squeezes between the mold halves. Trim this away with your hobby knife, **B**.

Before you cement anything, dry-fit all parts to ensure they mate properly. Sometimes a kit is warped — the parts don't line up properly. Glue the parts together in stages to fix this. First, glue the section that fits best and let it set completely (usually one hour). Next, carefully force the warped pieces together, apply glue, and hold them with spring-type clothespins, rubber bands, or small clamps. If the bonding surfaces of the parts have small irregularities that prevent a good fit, tape a sheet of sandpaper to a flat surface and rub the parts on the sheet a few times until they fit flush, **C**. Don't worry if you trim away the little alignment pegs; they may actually make it harder to get a good fit from a warped kit.

Apply cement to both surfaces to be joined, **D**. (If you're using liquid cement, see the box on page 45 for techniques.) The liquid may appear to evaporate, but don't worry; it's there, softening the plastic. Align the parts and squeeze them together. A thin bead of softened plastic should squish up along the joint as the parts chemically weld. Hold the assembly for 30 seconds to make sure things are set. A half minute is a long time; if you're not already doing it, try holding your breath that long. A good bond now will make for a strong model and happy modeler later on.

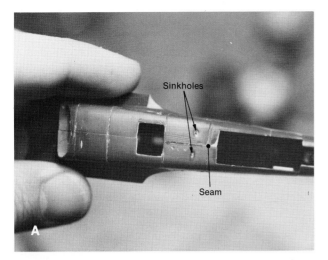

Sinkholes

Seam

A

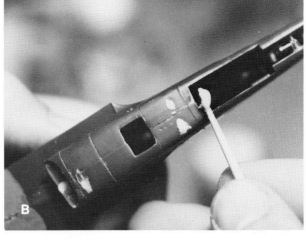

B

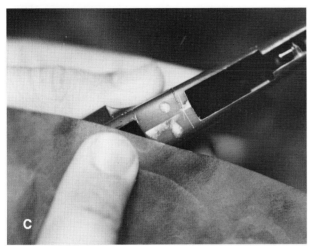

C

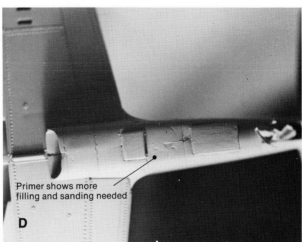

Primer shows more
filling and sanding needed

D

E

Step 2. Fill, sand, and prime. No matter how careful you are, you're liable to have a few small gaps between parts. These seams and sinkholes, small depressions in otherwise smooth surfaces, **A**, must be filled with putty. Put a dab of putty on the end of a toothpick and overfill the hole or seam, **B**. It takes time for the putty to dry — let the model set overnight and reacquaint yourself with your family. Next, sand the putty smooth with sandpaper or sanding film dipped in water, **C**. Wet sanding works faster and prevents the sandpaper from loading up with putty dust. Wipe off the residue with a cotton swab dipped in alcohol.

Use a primer to be sure you've done a good job of filling. The surface may look smooth, and may even feel smooth, but a bright light on a one-color surface will pop imperfections into view. I spray a coat of light gray paint over all the puttied areas. You'll be amazed how easy it is to see minor blemishes after a coat of primer, **D**. Odds are you'll find that you'll need another application of putty.

Fill, sand, and prime . . . fill, sand, and prime — the litany of modeling. With a little practice you'll get to the point where you won't be able to find the original seams.

Sometimes you'll have seams in areas that are too small to get at with sandpaper. Here, you can use white glue such as Elmer's Glue-All to fill small gaps. Mix one part white glue with three parts water and add a drop of liquid dishwashing detergent to break the surface tension of the water (this allows the mixture to flow better). Put a few drops of the mixture into the seam with a

medicine dropper. Capillary attraction will make the mixture flow the length of the depression. Now add full-strength white glue with a toothpick and it'll settle into the groove, **E**. Keep adding more until you've just slightly overfilled it, then wipe away the excess with a water-soaked cotton swab. There'll be some shrinkage as the glue dries, but it usually fills smoothly.

By now you should have something that looks like an airplane. The wings, fuselage, and tail are all assembled, filled, and primed, and the canopy, propeller, pilot figure, and drop tanks are conveniently stowed in plastic bags.

A

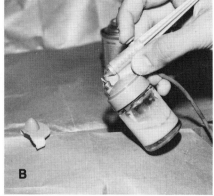

B

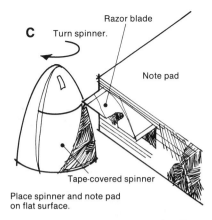

C Turn spinner. Razor blade

Note pad

Tape-covered spinner

Place spinner and note pad on flat surface.

Start the spray to the side of the model. Move your hand parallel to the surface of the model at an even speed.

Spray past the end of the model before releasing the spray button.

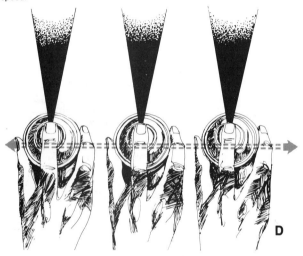

D

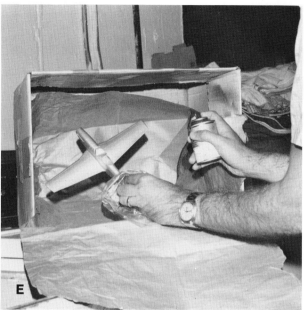

E

Step 3. Painting. The Testor Mustang kit came with decals for two aircraft. The more colorful one, "The Millie G," features green and yellow markings over aluminum. Although applying this colorful scheme would be more difficult, I decided it would be worth the effort. I also got to practice painting with brushes, spray cans, and airbrush.

It's easier to paint most of the little parts while they're still on the sprues, **A**, followed by a touch-up after they're cut off. That's what I did with the canopy frames, landing gear struts, and gear doors. I painted other pieces, like the prop assembly and drop tanks, as I went along.

A good rule is to paint the lightest color first. On this model, that was the white band on each horizontal stabilizer. Since there was little area to cover, I used the ¼" flat brush to apply Pactra Flat White (XF-2). After stirring the paint thoroughly, dip the brush into the bottle about halfway, and wipe off the excess paint on the inner lip of the bottle. Gently flow the paint from the brush onto the model surface, brushing in one direction, letting the paint settle naturally. If you try to work out brush marks, you will only make them worse. You're painting a miniature airplane, not a full-size barn. Enamels dry from the outside in, so excessive stroking will just smear the drying paint on top over the wet paint underneath. It may take a few coats to cover the dark green plastic; I needed three. I didn't worry about getting sharp lines to the white area since this would be masked later and bordered by green.

The yellow on the rudder and spinner was next. To make the yellow cover better, first spray on a coat of light gray primer. Painting the propeller spinner was a challenge — since the spinner has no flat surfaces, it would be difficult to mask the yellow band.

I airbrushed the entire spinner with Testor No. 1114 yellow. After stirring the paint, thin it three parts paint to one part Testor Enamel Thinner. This ratio worked well for this paint but is only a guideline — practice with different paints and thinning ratios to determine what's best for your airbrush. Place the flat end of the spinner on a loop of masking tape for a convenient holder, **B**. Between colors, I spray clean paint thinner through the airbrush and clean the tip with a pipe cleaner.

Let the spinner dry overnight, then cover it with a layer of frosty transparent tape. To cut out the mask for the yellow band, place a single-edge razor blade on a note pad, adjusting the height by the number of pages under the blade. Place the spinner and note pad on a flat surface, push the spinner against the blade and turn it, **C**, and carefully peel the tape from the tip of the spinner. After the green is painted and has dried, remove the tape on the yellow band. The base portion of the spinner is a separate piece and is painted green.

Most of my model is painted aluminum with a spray can, so I covered the cockpit, white stripes on the horizontal stabilizers, and yellow rudder with masking tape.

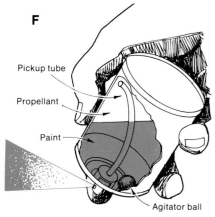

F

Pickup tube

Propellant

Paint

Agitator ball

When the can is held upside down, clear propellant expels paint from the pickup tube and nozzle.

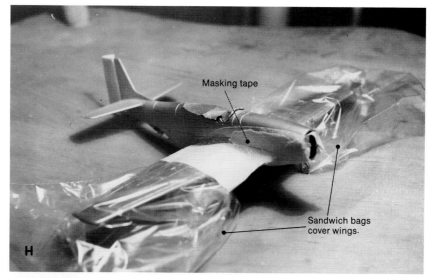

Masking tape

Sandwich bags cover wings.

H

Decal used as contour guide

G

I

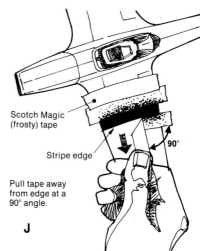

Scotch Magic (frosty) tape

Stripe edge

90°

Pull tape away from edge at a 90° angle.

J

Practice painting on a grocery bag inside your disposable spray booth, moving in and out until you find the distance where the paint covers uniformly but dries almost instantly. If the paint only mists, you're too far away; if it runs, you're too close. The correct distance will vary with the type of paint.

It's important to spray perpendicular to the surface of the model, **D**. If you turn the can from the wrist, you may have too much paint in the middle of the model and not enough at the ends. Swing your arm from your shoulder and start spraying before you get to the model — this prevents spatter at the start of the stroke. Continue spraying after you reach the other end of the model for the same reason, **E**. When you're done spraying, turn the can upside down, aim it into the box, and spray until no more color comes out, **F**. This clears the nozzle and prevents it from clogging.

With care, you'll be done in about five minutes. Set the model aside to let the paint harden for a day or two. It's completely set when you can't detect any wet paint smell. Leave the masking tape on because the dark green will be painted next.

The hardest part of this paint scheme is the curved demarcation between the silver and the green. Happily, Testor provides curved yellow decal stripes to separate the two colors. Carefully cut these out and trace their outlines onto masking tape stuck to a piece of glass, **G**. Then, following the instructions and box art, position the tape parallel to the panel lines on the nose and curve it down to the edge of the wing flap. Remember that you are covering the silver area below this line. Now mask off the rest of the model — use plastic sandwich bags instead of tape to cover the wings, **H**.

I used Testor Flat Beret Green for the upper fuselage and spinner color. It flows nicely with the ¼″ flat brush, but I decided to apply it with the airbrush.

Spray the paint perpendicular to the surface, just as you did with the spray can. When you are at the proper spraying distance, the paint should display a slight wet sheen on the model. As soon as the paint loses its sheen, peel off the masking tape, **I**. To touch up, spray a small puddle of paint on a piece of grocery bag and dip a 00 brush in it.

The last color is black. I used Pactra Flat Black (XF-1) for the tires, prop blades, and stripes on the wings. I used Scotch Magic tape (the frosty kind) to mask the stripes. If carefully applied, it won't pull up paint and, because it is thinner than masking tape, it reduces the paint's tendency to pile up at the edges. Lay the black on in one good stroke with the ¼″ brush. Remove the tape by pulling it away from the stripe's edge at a 90-degree angle, **J**.

Add the propeller, landing gear, and doors when the paint is dry. Leave off the canopy and windscreen, pilot, underwing tanks, and rocket tubes for now. Coat the entire model with Testor Glosscote after the cement has set, and stand by to decal.

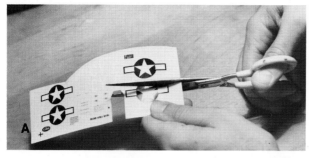

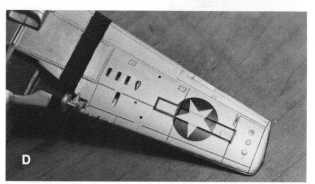

Step 4. Decals. Applying decals can be fun or it can be the worst part of the project. Testor's decals are good, but are thin and will tear if you aren't careful.

Cut the decal pieces out one at a time, as you need them, **A**. Dip each in warm water until the backing paper is soaked, usually five to ten seconds. Remove the decal from the water, uncurl it on a paper towel, and let it sit for about thirty seconds. This gives the adhesive time to dissolve, and gives you time to brush decal-setting solution on the spot where the decal will go. This softens the decal film and allows it to conform to rivets and panel lines.

Position the decal over its location and pull the paper out from under it, **B**. Gently align it with a brush and apply a final dose of setting solution, **C**. Don't touch the decals again until they're dry. Wrinkles and bubbles will appear in a few minutes, but don't panic — they'll eventually smooth out. After the decals are dry, pop the remaining bubbles with a pin and add more solvent to settle them down. When completely dry, the decals will snuggle down over the surface detail, **D**.

Apply decals to one side at a time and let them dry before flipping the model over (I learned the hard way that decals stick to fingers and thumbs as well as models). After waiting a day, gently wash away excess dried decal adhesive with a cotton swab dipped in setting solution. Once you're happy with everything, spray on a coat of Dullcote. The effect of this clear flat finish is magical — all the different paint colors and decals blend into one smooth, even surface! You'll have a model that looks like it has painted insignia instead of one that has a bunch of stickers glommed on it.

It's a good idea to try the Dullcote on a few extra decals applied to a scrap model first. Some European decals don't take well to oversprays.

Now, you may be asking why you use a gloss finish over flat paints, then a flat finish over the decals. You may have seen a model with decals that have frosty halos around them. These are caused by air trapped between the decal and the rough surface of flat paint. Using a gloss overcoat and trimming the decals as close to the ink as possible helps eliminate this. The flat overcoat helps to hide the edges, seals the decals to the surface, and cuts down on reflected light.

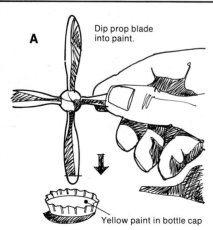

Dip prop blade into paint.

Yellow paint in bottle cap

Step 5. Final details. Regular plastic cements are the kiss of death for clear styrene — they craze the plastic and produce foggy blemishes. We get around this by gluing the windshield to the fuselage and the canopy to its frame with white glue. It dries clear and is strong enough to hold parts that won't be subject to stress. I also used white glue to attach the drop tanks and rocket launchers — it's easy to clean up excess glue with a wet cotton swab without harming the model's finish. Underwing stores are likely to be broken off, and the white glue bond yields before any damage is done to the parts.

An easy way to paint the prop blade tips is to dip each blade into a bottle cap containing a little yellow paint. Let the blades sit in the paint for about ten minutes so the paint gets a good grip. Then drain the excess paint by touching the blade to a paper towel. A second dip evens out any weak spots.

I'm pleased with my first try at a plastic airplane model as an adult. Even my wife and kids think it's pretty good, and they're not easily impressed. Maybe I'll enter it in an IPMS contest. Do they have a category for Rookie of the Year, or Comeback Modeler?

FSM

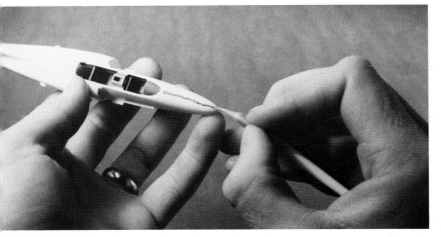

Fig. 5. The author applies a thin bead of putty to a seam with his homemade putty dispenser. It's inexpensive and easily cleaned after using.

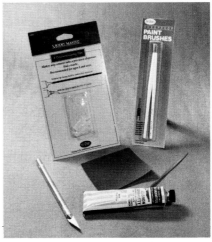

Fig. 1. All the tools you'll need to fill seams: Testor's glue tips and paintbrush make up the dispenser for putty. Excess putty can be removed with a knife and wet-or-dry sandpaper.

BASIC TECHNIQUES ✦ ADVANCED RESULTS

Seams like a breeze

An inexpensive putty dispenser simplifies modeling's most tedious chore

BY LANCE NORMAN

ONE OF MY early frustrations in building model aircraft was how long it took to fill and sand seams and joints. There just had to be a better, faster way to do this. After all, none of my modeling buddies show signs of insanity (other than an abundance of unbuilt kits).

While sitting at my work area one evening, a package of Testor's glue tips caught my eye. I wondered if I could get Squadron Green Putty to flow through them. With the glue tips, a small flat file, a Testor No. 8701 paintbrush, an X-acto knife, and 600-grit wet-or-dry sandpaper, Fig. 1, I came up with a reasonably quick way to fill seams.

Make a dispenser. I made my putty dispenser by cutting the Testor paintbrush to the length shown in Fig. 2. The brush handle becomes a plunger that fits inside the glue tip. You could also use a dowel in place of the brush handle.

Remove the cap from the tube of putty and hold the glue tip snug against the opening, Fig. 3. Gently squeeze the tube until the glue tip is half full. Next, insert your plunger into the back of the tip and push the putty toward the glue tip. Figure 4 shows how I cradle the dispenser in my hand while applying putty.

Filling seams and gaps. Filling seams and gaps is easy with this dispenser. Place the glue tip on the seam to be filled. Drawing your two fingers and thumb toward the palm of your hand starts the flow of putty. As you move the dispenser along the seam, a thin bead of putty fills the gaps, Fig. 5.

Because the bead of putty is so thin, you won't waste time sanding off excess putty. If you need a wider bead of putty, trim the tip with an X-acto knife.

I use a small flat file or a sharp blade to remove most of the putty. To finish I wet a small piece of 600-grit waterproof sandpaper and lightly sand the seam smooth.

Cleaning up. The beauty of filling seams this way is that there isn't much cleaning up to do. Just remove the plunger from the glue tip and wipe it clean with a paper towel. Let the putty in the glue tip dry, then pinch the tip with a pair of pliers and push the dried putty out of the tip with a pin.

See? No mess, no fuss, and the dispenser is totally reusable. Seams like a breeze to me! **FSM**

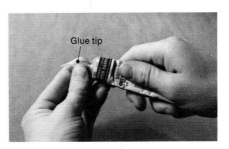

Glue tip

Fig. 3. Squadron Green Putty is squeezed into the glue tip — putty won't stick to the soft plastic tip.

Glue tip filled with putty

Paintbrush plunger

Fig. 4. The shortened paintbrush is used as a plunger to push the putty out the glue tip.

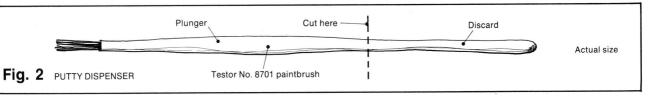

Plunger   Cut here   Discard

Actual size

Fig. 2 PUTTY DISPENSER   Testor No. 8701 paintbrush

The canopy on the author's 1/48 scale Monogram F-84F Thunderstreak blends beautifully with the fuselage. Note the sharp edges of the painted frame.

Fig. 2. Chris masks canopies with ⅛″ a[nd] ¼″ chart tape found in art-supply stores.

BASIC TECHNIQUES ◆ ADVANCED RESULTS

Masking and attaching canopies

Getting a clear edge on cockpit visibility

BY CHRISTOPHER BOWIE

MANY MODELERS SPEND lots of time detailing aircraft cockpits — the list of techniques and materials seems endless. However, even museum-quality cockpit detailing can be overshadowed by poor-fitting canopies and scratches and glue smears on the clear plastic.

After their initial experiences with tube glues and ruined canopies, some modelers switched to Microscale's Kristal-Kleer or another white glue (Tacky, Elmer's, Sobo, and so forth) to attach canopies. These water-based glues have advantages — they dry clear; they don't dissolve plastic, eliminating crazed clear parts; and mistakes can be cleaned up with a damp cloth.

However, white glues do have drawbacks. They don't hold the clear parts securely to the fuselage. Normally, the canopy/fuselage bond undergoes little stress, but if you need to blend a poor-fitting canopy to the fuselage with body putty, or if you like to mask and paint canopies after they're attached, you may find white glue inadequate. Filling, filing, and sanding the seam between canopy and fuselage can mar clear plastic irreparably. Removing masking tape can pull canopies right off the model if they're attached with white glue. Also, because white glue is not as hard as plastic, it can take on a different sheen when using buffable metallic paints such as Metalizer.

Try this. My simple method for attaching canopies provides a powerful bond between the clear parts and the fuselage, making cleanup less risky. I enjoy building jets of the 1950s with natural-metal finishes and colorful paint schemes, so these techniques are particularly helpful. My method involves chart tape and fast-drying liquid plastic cement.

If your finished model is to have the canopy closed, stuff damp bathroom tis-

sue around the cockpit before assem[bling] bling the fuselage. This seals off t[he] cockpit interior from overspray th[at] might be forced into the fusela[ge] through landing gear mounting hole[s,] wheel wells, and intakes. If oversp[ray] gets in, it may mar the inside of t[he] canopy. Minor seams around whe[el] wells can be sealed with white glue a[p]plied with a toothpick.

Carefully remove the clear par[ts] from the sprue with a sharp knife a[nd] test fit them to the fuselage. Use [a] piece of sandpaper wrapped around [a] small block of basswood or a needle fi[le] to shape the canopies for the best fit.

It's a good idea to keep clear parts i[n] a plastic sandwich bag to prevent acc[i]dental scratches, but if there a[re] scratches, rub them out with use [of] 1200-grit sandpaper. Wet the sandp[a]per and gently rub in a circular moti[on] over the scratched area. Next, pour [a] small amount of Brasso metal polis[h] ing compound onto a cotton rag, let [it] dry overnight, then polish the scratche[d] area with the dry compound. Next, ru[b] the canopy on your denim jeans for [a] few minutes, apply a thin coat of ca[r] wax, let it dry, and buff it with a ra[g.] Now your canopy should be perfect[ly] clear.

Lay strips of ⅛″-wide chart tape on [a] clear acrylic sheet cutting surfac[e.] (Acrylic won't dull your knife blades a[s] quickly as glass.) Cut pieces of ⅛″ tap[e] and overlap the edges of the clear are[a] of the canopy, Fig. 1. Cut off the exces[s] tape right on the canopy, leaving th[e] frame exposed. Cover the remainin[g] clear areas with ¼″-wide chart tap[e,] Fig. 2. I recommend matte chart tap[e] for masking; it has a low-tack adhe[sive, doesn't leave a residue, and is du[rable — the glossy chart tapes are to[o] sticky.

Paint the upper areas of the fuselag[e] which lie under the canopy and let th[e] paint dry thoroughly. Do any final de[tailing, such as attaching instrumen[t] panel coamings and head-up displays.

The moment of truth. Place th[e] masked canopy on the fuselage and ap[ply gentle pressure. Dip an inexpensiv[e]

Fig. 1 MASKING CANOPIES

Cover remainder of canopy with ¼″ chart tape

Exposed framing

Cut off ends with sharp blade

Mask edges with ⅛″ chart tape

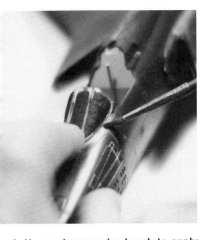

Fig. 3. Use an inexpensive brush to apply liquid cement. Capillary attraction draws the cement down the seam.

Fig. 4. When dry, the seam is sanded and filled as necessary. The chart tape protects the clear areas.

Fig. 5. If you plan open canopies, first shut them, seal them with white glue, then gently pop them off and reattach them in the open position.

paintbrush in quick-drying liquid plastic cement (such as IPS Weld-On #3 and #4, Micro Weld, or Tenax 7R), drain off the excess (the brush should be damp, not dripping), and run the brush along the seam, Fig. 3. Capillary attraction will draw the cement into the seam and chemically bond the clear parts to the fuselage. The chart tape masking prevents the cement from clouding the clear areas of the canopy. Remember, use the cement sparingly — you can always apply more cement if needed, but it is difficult to repair the damage caused by too much.

When the cement is dry, clean up the seam with a file and 400-grit wet-or-dry sandpaper, Fig. 4. The durable chart tape will prevent damage to the clear areas. If there are any gaps, fill them with putty or gap-filling super glue and sand again. Next, paint a thin coat of flat aluminum on the seam to help spot flaws and correct them. The wrong bond permits the serious seam work needed on some kits.

When you're happy with the seam, sand it with 600-grit sandpaper and you're ready to paint. If you have open canopies, stuff damp tissue paper into the cockpit and inside the canopies, then attach them in the closed position with white glue. When you're done painting, remove the chart tape and do the final assembly. For open canopies, gently pop them off and reattach them in the open position, Fig. 5.

Some aircraft kits have clear parts that blend right into the fuselage without framing. You'll lose up to $1/16''$ of the clear portion when attaching the canopy, but most canopies on real aircraft have a colored putty or fiberglass insulation at the joint that can be simulated with solid-color decal strips.

I hope these techniques help you successfully tackle one of the most difficult — and critical — areas on model aircraft. **FSM**

SOURCES

Chart (or graphic) tape is available at most art supply stores. Look for these quick-drying cements at hobby shops:
● IPS Weld-On #3 and #4: Industrial Polychemical Service, P. O. Box 471, Gardena, CA 90247
● Micro Weld: Microscale Industries, 1555 Placentia Ave., Newport Beach, CA 92663
● Tenax 7R: Hebco Enterprises, Spencerport, NY 14559

Terry's 1/35 scale Panzer IB was built straight from the box (it's a Testor/Italeri kit). The model features a simple, one-color paint scheme, making it an ideal first tank project. Note how dry-brushing highlights the edges of panels and bolt heads, emphasizing the raised detail and adding a realistic armor texture.

BASIC TECHNIQUES ◆ ADVANCED RESULTS

Fig. 1. Three good candidates for your first tank kit (all 1/35 scale), left to right: Testor/Italeri Panzer IB, Tamiya Japanese Chi-Ha, and Testor/Italeri Hetzer tank destroyer. The main difference among the models is the complexity of the paint schemes, with the Panzer the simplest and the "ambush" pattern on the Hetzer the most complex.

Building your first tank kit

Assembly is easy — the emphasis is on painting techniques

BY TERRY SUNDAY

*Y*OU'VE DECIDED to build a tank kit. Good! There's never been a better selection of armor models available than you'll find today, and a stroll through your local hobby shop will reveal a wide variety of armored vehicle kits in all scales, shapes, and sizes.

The hints, tips, and techniques in this article will help you build your first tank kit, whether you're new to the hobby or just want a change of pace from aircraft or automobiles. We'll concentrate on building a kit straight from the box, and our project will be split up into three phases: assembly, painting, and decaling.

Assembly is easy and straightforward, because armor models usually have no moving parts or complex curved surfaces, and the kit parts tend to be robust and forgiving. You'll spend most of your time painting — depending on the complexity of the paint scheme, as much as 75 percent of it. Finally, tanks usually have few markings, so decaling doesn't take long.

Tank kits come in 1/76, 1/72, 1/48, 1/35, and 1/24 scales, and there are a few in even larger sizes. For your first project I recommend a 1/35 scale model, Fig. 1. This is a good size to work on, neither too big nor too small. Most recent 1/35 scale kits are accurate, highly detailed, and fit together well. So grab a kit and let's get started!

A plan of attack — by subassem-

blies. As you assemble your kit, always keep in mind how you will paint it so you can plan construction steps accordingly. Most instruction sheets call for assembling the suspension and road wheels right away and adding them to the hull, but it's better to divide the vehicle into subassemblies, paint each one separately, then add the running gear as the last or next-to-last step.

For a typical tank, the turret and the hull will each be a subassembly, and on vehicles with complex suspensions each sprung unit with its road wheels can be a separate subassembly. Attach all the parts that will be painted the basic vehicle color (hatches, lifting rings, storage boxes, grab handles, and so on), but leave off tools, lights, towing cables, exhaust pipes, and other parts that will be painted differently. Attach these after the main vehicle is painted but before dry-brushing (more on that later).

Assembly techniques. Most of the rules to follow in assembling armor kits apply to other plastic kits as well. First, remove all mold lines. Nearly every part will have a ridge around it where the halves of the mold came together. The line on some parts will be barely noticeable; on others it may be pronounced. Depending on the part, sand, file, or scrape away the mold lines with a modeling knife.

Road wheels often have prominent mold lines, Fig. 2, and removing them can be tedious, but if neglected the lines will be glaringly obvious when

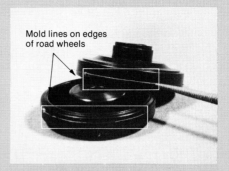

Fig. 2. Before you cement anything together, take the time to remove mold lines, such as the ridges on these road wheels from a Japanese Type 74 tank, by carefully filing, scraping, or sanding.

your model is painted and dry-brushed. Take your time and make sure all traces of the lines are removed.

Choosing glues. You'll need two adhesives to build plastic armor kits, Fig. 3. For general assembly use liquid styrene cement. Simply hold the parts together, touch the joint with a brush filled with cement, and capillary action will draw enough cement into the joint to make a strong bond. A second application after the first has dried will make the joint even stronger. Try for neatness as you apply the cement, but don't worry if a little slops onto areas adjacent to the joint — as long as you don't touch or mar the surface while the cement is wet, the spots will disappear under your first coat of paint. To

Fig. 3. You won't need many tools to build your first tank — liquid plastic cement, super glue, a modeling knife with several new blades, small files, and tweezers. In addition you'll need paint and brushes, but that's it.

Fig. 4. On this Chi-Ha the main gun barrel was molded with a bored-out muzzle, but the machine gun barrel was solid. Drilling out the smaller barrel with a modeling knife adds realism. Note the rust streaks from some of the hull bolts.

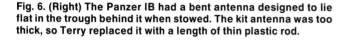

.020" sheet plastic
to enclose sponson

Fig. 5. The open area under the sponson of this Chi-Ha has been boxed in with sheet plastic. If not corrected the gaping void would have been an obvious defect in the model.

Fig. 6. (Right) The Panzer IB had a bent antenna designed to lie flat in the trough behind it when stowed. The kit antenna was too thick, so Terry replaced it with a length of thin plastic rod.

attach tiny parts, use a No. 00 or smaller paintbrush instead of the coarse brush in the bottle lid.

Cyanoacrylate adhesives, often called "super glues," will also come in handy. These strong, fast-setting glues are ideal for attaching flexible plastic tracks and for adding non-plastic parts. (Cyanoacrylates will also glue your fingers together, so handle them with care.) Don't use the tiny applicator tubes that come with some types of cyanoacrylate; instead, unscrew the cap and dip a toothpick, a piece of thin sprue (the "tree" of plastic that holds molded parts together), or other surplus plastic into the glue to extract a drop at a time.

Opening gun barrels. Tanks usually have guns bristling from their hulls and turrets. On recent kits, the main cannon muzzles (at least the last ⅛" or

so) are hollow, realistically simulating the bore, Fig. 4. Some older kits have solid cannon tubes, and machine-gun barrels are always solid, since a scale-size muzzle opening would be virtually impossible to mold. Drilling out the solid barrels will enhance your model, and it's not hard to do.

Using a new No. 11 modeling knife blade, carefully rotate the point against the end of the barrel with gentle pressure until a hole is carved out. Use a brand-new blade, because the point will either break off or become dull almost immediately, and a dull or broken point will make it impossible to center the bore. Careful is the watchword here: It takes little pressure to carve the hole, and too much force will make the blade slip and damage the barrel — or you!

Suspension assembly. Some tank kits come with working suspension, usually consisting of many tiny parts. Such parts are fragile, often out of scale, and frequently difficult to align properly. I prefer to defeat the working feature and cement the suspension parts solidly in place. To ensure the suspension is level, cement all the road wheel arms or bogies in place, then gently press the hull down on a firm flat surface (a tabletop works fine) before the cement dries. Level the suspension front to back and side to side. (Whether you do this before or after painting depends on the kit you're building.)

One shortcoming common to many tank kits is that the undersides of the sponsons (the parts of the hull directly above the tracks) are left open. These open areas can be obvious, especially if the tank lacks side armor skirts or if there is a large space above the tracks. The solution is to box in the open area with .020" sheet plastic, Fig. 5. Your hobby shop should have the plastic you'll need; cut the pieces oversize, then carefully trim them to shape, checking the fit frequently. Fill small gaps with filler putty, also available from your hobby shop.

Filling gaps. Also use plastic putty to fill small gaps between hull plates and wherever the kit parts don't fit exactly right. Don't worry too much about neatness, because most of the plates of tanks are anything but neat. The important thing is to close up gaps that would allow you to see into the model.

My only other assembly tip concerns antennas. If your kit provides a molded whip antenna, chances are it will be far too thick. Some kits don't include antennas, but provide instructions for making them from stretched sprue. However, stretched sprue has an an

Steel color
on sprocket
teeth and
track guides

Fig. 7. Dry-brush the drive sprockets and track guides with Steel or silver to simulate bare metal where the paint has worn off, but don't overdo the effect.

ying habit of warping and twisting — after a few weeks or months you may end up with an antenna that looks like it's being blown around by a hurricane! A better idea is to use thin plastic rod, purchased from your hobby shop. This material lacks the realistic taper of stretched sprue, but it will stand up straight. Drill a small hole in the antenna mounting base, just as you did to hollow the ends of the machine gun barrels, and attach the replacement antenna, Fig. 6.

Painting. The quality of the finish makes or breaks an armor model, and the most important painting rule can be stated in two words: *paint everything*. It doesn't matter if the color of the plastic *exactly* matches the color scheme you plan to use, because unpainted plastic, no matter how you try to disguise it, always looks like plastic. Tank paint schemes range from a single overall color to complex patterns; I strongly recommend choosing a one-color scheme for your first kit.

The best way to apply paint is with an airbrush, and to my way of thinking, an airbrush is the second best modeling investment you can make — right behind a modeling knife with a handful of No. 11 blades. The first time you use one you'll be converted. You don't have to buy an expensive air compressor at first (the compressor costs several times more than the airbrush); instead, you can get by for a while with relatively inexpensive cans of compressed propellant.

If you don't have an airbrush, the next best way to paint your model is with a brush. Small cans of spray paint are a poor third. The problem with spray cans is that the spray is either full on or completely off. You have no control over the amount of paint that comes out when you press the button. Lacking this control, you're likely to get blobs of paint where you don't want them, runs, ripples, or worse.

A lot of modelers wash completed models in a gentle detergent solution to remove greasy residue and finger oils the paint will adhere. Maybe so, but I've never had a problem getting paint to adhere to armor models. Unless your model has a noticeably greasy surface, washing it before painting shouldn't be necessary.

First paint each subassembly with the basic overall color. I normally leave the road wheels attached to the molding trees for painting, making it easy to zap each one with a quick blast from the airbrush. Let all painted parts dry thoroughly — this is critical, because the easiest way to ruin a paint job is to apply a wash before the base coat is dry. I always let the base coat dry at least three days, sometimes as much as a week.

Applying a wash. If you stop painting after applying the basic color to your tank, it will look flat and lifeless. The secret to realism lies in applying washes, then dry-brushing.

A wash is nothing more than diluted enamel paint. When you brush it on, the thinned color is drawn into corners, crevices, and recessed areas, creating a shadow effect without noticeably changing the base color. You'll have to experiment to determine the proper dilution, since it depends on the colors and the brand of paint and thinner you choose, but a good starting point is 1 part paint to 9 parts thinner. Darken your basic color with a little dark brown or black, then thin it and apply it to the entire model with a wide, soft brush. If you apply too much, dab — don't rub — away the excess with a soft cloth.

After applying the wash the tank will look absolutely horrible! Your smoothly applied base coat will be a mottled, blotchy mess, probably with several glossy patches. Don't worry — by the time you apply the last finish coat, the model will be amazingly, and realistically, transformed.

Dry-brushing techniques. Let the wash dry for a day or so before dry-brushing. The secret of dry-brushing is to never, *ever* dip the paint directly from the bottle. Instead, put a few drops of your base color on an index card, add a drop or two of flat white, and mix with a toothpick. The paper will soak most of the oil out of the paint, leaving the pigment behind. The thickened paint will dry quickly and you'll have to replenish it often, but for a few minutes its consistency will be perfect for dry-brushing.

Choose a fairly wide, short-bristled brush that's absolutely dry (don't use one that you've just cleaned; it will leave streaks on the model). Dip the tip in the thickened paint and stroke the brush across the card until almost all the paint is removed. Holding the brush perpendicular to the model, gently scrub the bristles over the surface. Easy does it — don't use much pressure. Soon you'll see raised details start to lighten as they collect tiny amounts of paint, Fig. 7.

Once you've gone over the entire model, mix a slightly lighter shade of paint and dry-brush again, concentrating on the upper surfaces of the tank. You can continue lightening the paint and dry-brushing until the results look good to you, but two or three passes are usually enough.

Tricks with tracks. Remove the road wheels from the molding tree, file off the mold lines, and finish painting the wheels. If the wheels on the tank you are modeling have rubber tires (not all do) paint the rubber portions with a mixture of flat black and Panzer Gray. The proportions are not important, and varying the mix from wheel to wheel adds realism. Skewer each wheel on the handle of an old paintbrush to hold it while painting, then dry-brush the road wheels just as you did the rest of the tank, but don't use quite as much white.

Paint both sides of the tracks with the basic body color and let them dry. Then apply a wash of black, dark brown, or dark gray-green, depending on the hull color. Dry-brush first with the basic color, lightened just a little, then with Steel. Finally, add touches of Rust around the connecting links (not on the running surfaces). Don't overdo the rust — a little goes a long way.

Fig. 8. Upper portions of track should sag realistically. Place a drop of super glue between the track and return roller, then hold the track down until the glue sets.

Fig. 9. The last step in building your first tank is overspraying it with a coat of clear flat finish to "homogenize" the surface and deaden shiny spots. Terry used an airbrush to apply the main areas of color on the complex ambush paint scheme of this Hetzer, then dabbed on the oval-shaped tan spots with a small brush.

Also, dry-brush a little steel on the teeth of the drive sprockets to simulate bare metal beneath worn-off paint.

I prefer bonding track ends with super glue to using the heated screwdriver called for in most instruction sheets. However, some tracks are made of plastic that can't be bonded with super glue. If you use a heated screwdriver, make sure the pins are flattened well; they can stretch, and the tracks may eventually come apart if the joint is not tight.

Some flexible tracks exude an oily mold release agent which prevents paint from adhering well. The oily film is almost impossible to remove: I've tried soap and water, alcohol, enamel thinner, turpentine, and other solvents, usually without success. The solution is to paint the tracks as well as you can, flex them as little as possible during installation (every bend will make some paint flake off), then touch them up after they are secured in place.

Making tracks sag. An important characteristic of most tanks is sagging tracks. Real track shoes are heavy, and the upper run of track sags between the return rollers. You can create realistic sag by tying the track down using thin black thread, but the thread may be visible.

A better way is to use super glue. Pick up a drop of glue on a toothpick and touch it to the top of a return roller (or the top of a road wheel on tanks without return rollers) and the underside of the track. Gently squeeze the track around the roller until the cement sets, Fig. 8. When you release the pressure, the track will rebound just the right amount and you'll end up with an upper run of track that looks as if it weighs a ton. Tracks that can't be super glued will require the thread treatment, but whatever you do, don't leave the upper track floating weightlessly above the wheels.

Applying decals. You now have an assembled, painted, and dry-brushed tank, and the next step is to apply the kit decals. Armored vehicles usually carry little more than national insignia, unit markings, and vehicle numbers; at most the decals may include a few special symbols such as bridge classification discs, crew names, and (on World War II Russian tanks) revolutionary signs.

The article that begins on page 98 of this book explains decaling in detail and I have only one note to add. While you don't have to apply a gloss coat to the whole tank, it's best to gloss complete panels or hull plates where markings will be placed, because the difference in the reflectivity of areas that you gloss coat will be noticeable even after the final flat finish is applied. Making the boundaries of the glossed areas coincide with joints or panel lines is a good way to disguise the difference.

After the decals and setting agent have dried, dry-brush the decal surfaces to blend the markings into the paint scheme and soften the edges. Then it's time for the final finishing step—a clear matte spray. This flat coating will even up the reflectivity of the entire model and the mottling will disappear, Fig. 9.

The best way to apply flat finish is with an airbrush. Dilute the finish a little as possible, just enough to get it to go through the airbrush (the more you dilute the matte finish, the less matte it becomes). It's important to use fresh thinner, preferably the kind especially made for airbrushes. Mask transparent areas such as vision blocks, headlights, and searchlight lenses before you spray.

So there you have it, your first armor model. Now that you're started, your skills will improve with each kit you tackle, and as your results improve you'll find that armor modeling offers enough challenges to keep you building for years! **FSM**

Bill's Hardee's Monte Carlo model features a completely plumbed and wired engine, cockpit improvements, and Fred Cady Design decals.

Modeling a NASCAR Winston Cup winner

Detailing Monogram's 1/24 scale Monte Carlo stocker

Y BILL COULTER
HOTOS BY JOHN COULTER

W INSTON CUP NASCAR stock cars are popular subjects for auto odelers, especially since Monogram roduces 1/24 scale kits of most of the dy styles in current competition. hey're excellent kits, but attention to tail can easily turn a ho-hum, out-of- e-box model into a surprisingly accu- te replica.

200 mph airborne! The subject for my odel is the 1983 Chevrolet Monte arlo SS sponsored by Hardee's res- urants and driven by three-time ASCAR champion and four-time Day- na 500 winner Cale Yarborough.

In 1981, Yarborough joined forces ith builder Harry Ranier and raced uicks. In 1983, they switched to the ewly introduced Monte Carlo SS. rew chief Wadell Wilson had the or- ge and white Chevy humming dur-

ing practice for the 1983 Daytona 500.

During qualifying, Cale opened his assault on the pole position with the first official 200-mph lap in the track's history. Entering turn three of the second lap on the 2½-mile, high-banked speedway, the right rear tire began to trail smoke, a telltale indicator of a car losing traction.

Yarborough frantically tried to correct the 200-mph, 3,700-pound missile, but air rushing under the car launched it into a series of barrel rolls. The wrecked racer finally came to rest in the grass, amazingly right-side up.

Uninjured but shaken, Yarborough was forced to start a backup car far back in the field instead of the pole position. Despite all the adversity, car number 28 visited victory lane as the winner of the 1983 Daytona 500. It also was the first time that a TV camera showed the checkered flag from inside the winning race car.

It was a good year for the Hardee's

team. Running a limited schedule of only 16 events, they won at Daytona and Charlotte, and twice at Michigan.

Start 'er up. To build Yarborough's Hardee's stock car, you'll need a Monogram 83-85 notch-back Monte Carlo (kit No. 2245 or 2299) and the Hardee's decals from Fred Cady Design (sheet No. 606). You'll also need a pin vise, motor tool, small-diameter drill bits, coarse sandpaper, tweezers, a 00 or 000 paintbrush, and a sharp hobby knife.

For supplies, you'll need small-diameter coated and uncoated wire, silver craft braid (⅟₃₂″, ⅟₁₆″, and ³⁄₃₂″ diameters), white glue, super glue, a straight pin, transparent blue and transparent red paint, flat white water-based paint, ⅛″ shrink tubing, masking tape, thin sheet styrene, and ⅟₁₆″ Chartpak tape. The silver braid can be found in craft stores.

I've organized the project into steps to make it easier to build. Pay close attention to the accompanying photos and drawings.

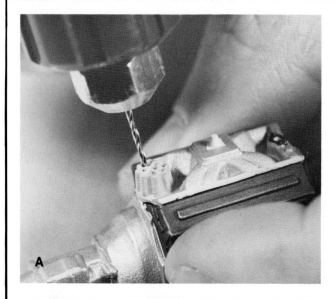

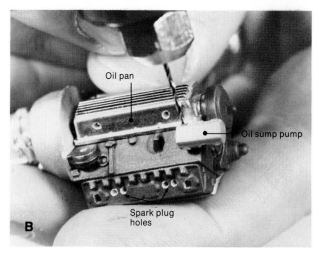

B

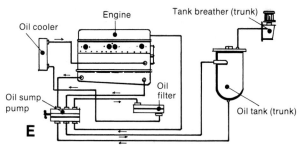

E

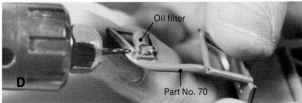

D

F

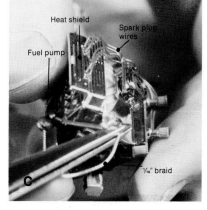

C

Step 1. Plumbing the engine. Much of this work is done with a motor tool. Caution: Operate the motor tool at low speeds, since high-speed drilling and grinding will melt styrene.

First, use a small-diameter bit to drill nine spark plug and coil wire holes in the top of the distributor (**A**). You'll also need to drill holes in the engine block for the other end of the spark plug wires (**B**). Follow that with corresponding holes drilled in the heat shields next to the valve covers (**C**).

A ¹⁄₁₆″ bit is used to drill the following holes: the rear surface of the left valve cover; both ends of the left side of the oil pan (**B**); three holes through the sump pump on the left front corner of the engine block (**B**); one hole laterally through the oil filter (**D**); top and bottom hose connections for the oil cooler where it attaches to the radiator; one hole in the base of the overflow tank on the right side of the fire wall; one hole in the upper right front corner of the radiator; and finally two holes into the outlets of the dual master cylinders located on the left side of the fire wall.

Run small-diameter coated wire from the distributor to each spark plug hole (**C**). The fuel pump wasn't molded on the kit's otherwise well-detailed small block GM V-8. I found one in my scrap box and epoxied it in place on the lower front corner of the engine block (**C**). Drill a ¹⁄₁₆″ hole horizontally through the pump, then run braid from the carburetor down the right front side of the engine through the fuel pump, into a hole in the lower right corner of the fire wall, and back through the rear bulkhead to the fuel tank.

Run ¹⁄₁₆″ braid from the coolant overflow tank on the fire wall to the hole in the upper right corner of the radiator. The ³⁄₃₂″ braid is used for the top and bottom radiator hoses.

Use ¹⁄₁₆″ braid to plumb the oil system following the schematic (**E**). The oil sump pump (**B**) is the brick-shaped unit on the oil pan (part No. 48), the oil cooler (**F**) is next to the radiator (No. 47), the oil filter (**D**) is on the front end of the left chassis frame (No. 70), and the oil tank (**F**) is the large cylinder on the trunk floor (No. 18).

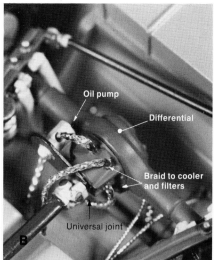

A — Rear end oil cooler (part No. 16) / Oil filters / 1/16" braid through bulkhead to rear end

B — Oil pump / Differential / Braid to cooler and filters / Universal joint

Step 2. Rear end. The rear end oil is cooled and filtered on stock cars. The kit provides the cooler (part No. 16), but I scratchbuilt the filters and pump. The cooler and filters (**A**) are mounted behind the driver's seat in the cockpit, while the pump (**B**) is attached between the universal joint and the differential. I used 1/16" braid to plumb the rear end according to the schematic (**C**). Sketch **D** shows how to make the differential pump from sheet styrene and sprue.

Paint every joint where a braid mates with an accessory; the ends of each braid should be painted transparent red, and the fittings on the accessories painted transparent blue.

Two lengths of log chain are used as safety retainers for the rear end and truck-arm assembly on stock cars. Use inexpensive jewelry chain attached to fine wire eyelets on either side of the differential and to the lateral chassis cross member (**E**).

Next come the brake lines running from the master cylinder on the fire wall to a hole in each disk brake caliper (**F**). The line to the rear brakes runs through the lower right corner of the rear bulkhead to a T fitting on the top of the rear axle (**E**). Paint the recesses of the front coil springs flat black to improve their appearance (**G**).

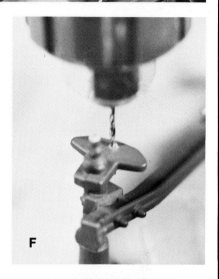

F

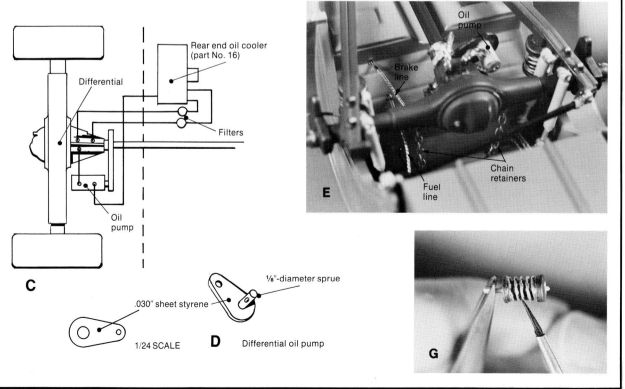

C — Differential / Rear end oil cooler (part No. 16) / Filters / Oil pump

D — .030" sheet styrene / 1/8"-diameter sprue / 1/24 SCALE / Differential oil pump

E — Oil pump / Brake line / Chain retainers / Fuel line

G

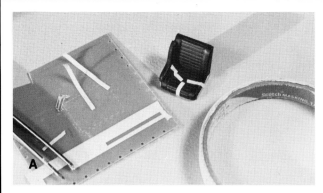

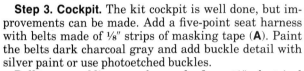

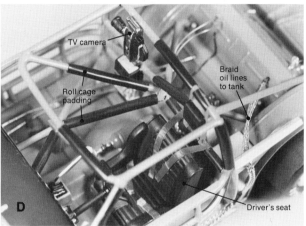

Step 3. Cockpit. The kit cockpit is well done, but improvements can be made. Add a five-point seat harness with belts made of ⅛″ strips of masking tape (**A**). Paint the belts dark charcoal gray and add buckle detail with silver paint or use photoetched buckles.

Roll cage padding can be made from ⅛″ electrical shrink tubing. Cut the tubing to length, carefully slit each piece diagonally, then slip it onto the roll cage (**B**). You may need to use super glue to keep the tubing on the roll cage.

Fashion the driver's protective window netting from horizontal and vertical strips of ¹⁄₁₆″ chart tape laid out on a ⅛″ grid. The finished net measures 1″ x ¾″ and is draped out of the driver's window (**C**).

The finished cockpit features the video camera mount included in the kit. Improve it by painting it black and silver (**D**).

Step 4. Wheels and tires. Sand the tread of the tires with a coarse grade of sandpaper to simulate wear (**A**). Next, paint the raised letters with a fine brush and flat white water-based paint (**B**).

Flat black applied to the recesses of the wheels adds realism. Next, drill a small hole in each wheel rim and insert ⅛″ sections of straight pin to simulate the valve stems. Paint the valves black with silver tips and attach them with a tiny drop of super glue.

Wheel-balancing weights can be added by applying a small drop of white glue to the wheel rim edge with a toothpick. When they're dry, paint them gunmetal with one small strip of chrome in the center.

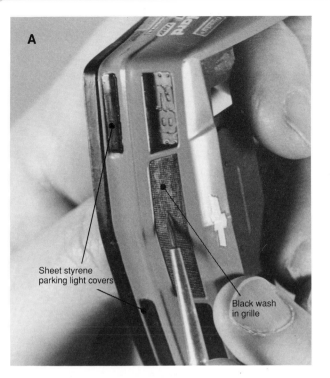

A

Sheet styrene parking light covers

Black wash in grille

B

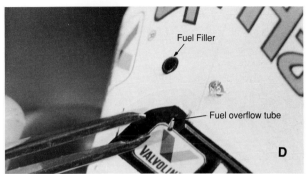

Fuel Filler

Fuel overflow tube

D

Masking tape retainers

Two-way radio antenna

C

radio antenna from a small piece of sprue and a $^{7}/_{16}''$-long piece of guitar string or fine wire.

Place a $^{1}/_{8}''$ section of straight pin in the upper left corner of the rear taillight panel for the fuel system overflow tube (**D**).

Referring to photos of real Winston Cup stock cars, you could add many other details to your model. How about a crankcase, dipstick, throttle linkage, detailed driver figure, steering front end, or opening trunk lid? The only limitations are time and your imagination. **FSM**

SOURCES

● Fred Cady decals: Fred Cady Design, Inc., P.O. Box 576, Mt. Prospect, IL 60056
● Photoetched seat belt buckles: Model Technologies, 2761 Saturn, Unit E, Brea, CA 92621

Step 5. Body details. Cover the parking light recesses on the front bumper with thin sheet styrene painted flat black (**A**), and use a wash of flat black to produce a realistic grille. Improve the retainer cables for the hood pin clips by drill

ing out the kit eyelets, bending fine uncoated wire into a loop and gluing both ends into each hole (**B**).

Use small squares of masking tape to attach the front windshield (**C**), then paint them either gunmetal or silver. Make the two-way

Building your first waterline ship kit

1/700 scale ship models are easy to build and detail

BY DENNIS MOORE

OF ALL THE PLASTIC SHIP models currently on the market, 1/700 scale waterline kits top the list in popularity and availability. Over the years, Tamiya, Aoshima, Fujimi, Hasegawa, Matchbox, and Testor/Italeri have produced most of the World War Two-vintage ships of the Japanese Navy, as well as several classes of American, English, and German vessels.

Waterline kits have the advantage of being small, allowing you to store lots of them on the shelf, and since they don't have complete hulls (nothing below the waterline is molded), you don't have to worry about stands. What is a waterline? That's the line painted on the ship's hull that corresponds to the surface of the water when the ship is normally loaded and on an even keel (level, not tilting).

The model I assembled for this article is Tamiya's 1/700 scale Imperial Japanese Navy light cruiser *Kuma* (kit No. 7780). She was built just after World War One, and after modifications, soldiered on until sunk by the Allies in the Strait of Malacca in January 1944.

Building a ship kit is like any other type of modeling; patience, a little research, and planning pay off in the appearance of the finished product. Even casual builders are interested in making accurate models, but good, affordable reference books are few and far between. Try your central public library or a university library. You may be pleasantly surprised with what you find. For instance, *Warships of the Imperial Japanese Navy, 1869-1945*, by Jentschura, Jung, and Mickel (Naval Institute Press, 1976), provided me with most of my information on the

Kiso class of which the *Kuma* is a member.

Tamiya's kit represents the *Kuma* as she looked between her 1935 refit and the start of WWII. Like other Tamiya waterline kits, it's a good choice for novice ship builders because it has many of the same components found on larger and more expensive kits.

Getting started. Although the kit instructions suggest working on many of the smaller components first, I always begin with a ship's largest structure, the hull. Begin by removing all mold marks from the bow and stern — any model will look better without extra flash, mold parting seams, and eject pin depressions. Use 400-grit wet-or-dry sandpaper, a motor tool, or the handy little Flex-i-file, which is great for getting into corners. I cut the Flex-i-file bands in half to make them even more useful, Fig. 1.

Adding even a little extra detail can greatly enhance the look of a model. I add anchor chains in place of the ones molded onto the bow. Hobby shops

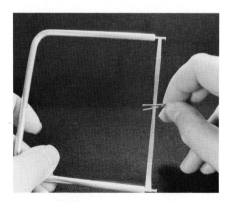

Fig. 1. A Flex-i-file belt that has been cut in half is passed through part of the forward tripod mast to remove mold marks.

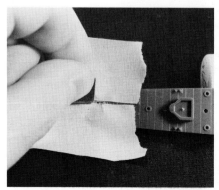

Fig. 2. Dennis uses masking tape to cover surrounding deck detail while removing the molded-in anchor chains.

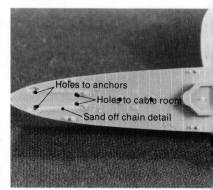

Fig. 3. The lower molded-in chain has been sanded away and holes have been drilled for the new chain.

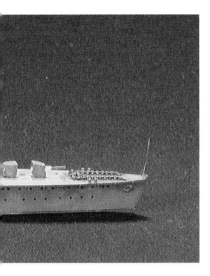

The author's completed Tamiya 1/700 scale *Kuma* is a good kit for starting a collection of waterline ship models. It's easy to build and, with a few added details, is an excellent replica. A close-up shows many of the details Dennis added: blast bags to the guns, covers on the life-boats, and pastel weathering to the sides of the hull.

specializing in model railroading usually carry miniature chain. I use Campbell No. 256 chain; a package provides enough for several ship kits. To remove the molded-on anchor chain, place masking tape around it so that you don't accidentally sand into the deck, Fig. 2. It's not necessary to obliterate every last vestige of the molded chain since the replacement will cover the area anyway.

To accommodate the chain, drill holes in the deck where each chain goes into the cable room (aft) and out to the anchor (fore), Fig. 3. The cable room holes should be drilled completely through the deck, while the holes to the anchor need to be deep enough to accept only the end of the chain. Cut the chain to length and cement it in place with a white glue such as Elmer's, Fig. 4.

The superstructure and other metal areas of Japanese ships were painted dark gray — I use Pactra International Colors Naval Dark Gray. Check the painting instructions that come with the kit to determine what areas should be gray. I like Pactra's Panzer Yellow for the wood areas. When preparing to paint the deck of a 1/700 scale vessel, determine if it's easier to airbrush or hand paint — the number and design of deck hatches, small deck houses, and other projections will make the difference. If you're going to hand paint the deck tan, use Polly S Earth Yellow — you'll have fewer brush marks than with enamels, and touching up with a second coat will be easier.

This ship's deck isn't too cluttered, so

Fig. 4. Dennis carefully positions the tiny chain, then attaches it with white glue.

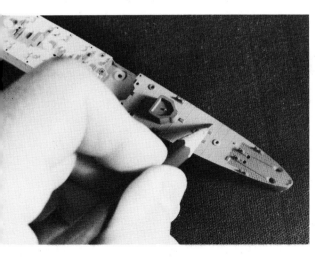

Fig. 5. A soft lead or art pencil is used to accent the raised deck plank lines.

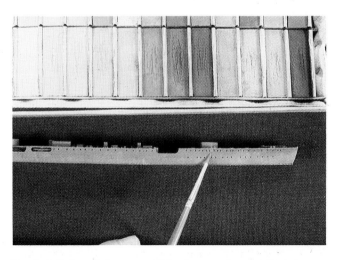

Fig. 6. Artist pastels are used to show rust and salt stains on the hull.

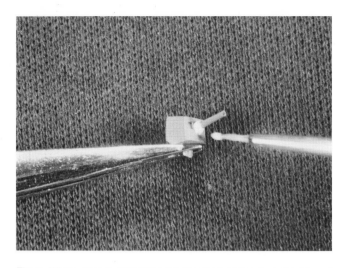

Fig. 7. White glue is painted onto the face of the gun shield and around the gun barrel to form the blast bag.

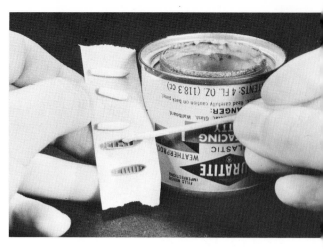

Fig. 8. To make them easier to handle, place the lifeboats on piece of masking tape. Dennis fills the boats with putty applie with a toothpick, then sands them smooth.

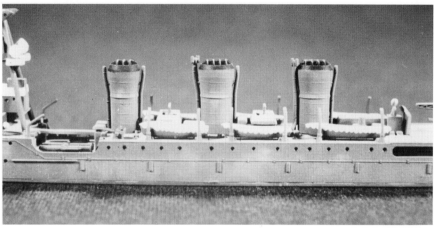

Fig. 9. The covers on the lifeboats are painted white. Note the canvas covers over the searchlights on the tripod mast.

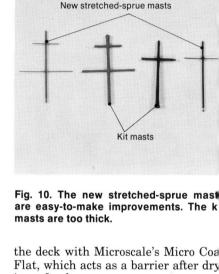

Fig. 10. The new stretched-sprue mast are easy-to-make improvements. The k masts are too thick.

Fig. 12. White glue fills the gaps between the searchlight platform and the tripod mast.

I used an airbrush and masked off the areas as I went along. Unfortunately, some structures can't be masked perfectly, and touching up the gray topside with a paintbrush is in order. Before hand brushing your touch-ups, make sure that the hull's paint dries for several days — if not cured completely, enamels tend to lift when new paint is applied. If you're in a rush, overspray the deck with Microscale's Micro Coa Flat, which acts as a barrier after dry ing a few hours.

After all the paint is dry, I sta weathering and accenting the hull. Th raised lines on the deck represent th spaces between planks or deck lino leum. To accent them, I run the side a soft lead pencil lightly over the line Fig. 5. Take care not to mark the dec planks, but some touch-up will proba bly be necessary.

Because of their dark color, Japanes warship hulls were usually discolore by salt spray. Salt spray and rust ca be simulated with artist's chalk pas tels, available at art supply stores an some hobby shops. Pastels are excel lent for producing all sorts of weather ing effects on ships, armor, or aircraf Because of the small scale, I use a 00 paintbrush to apply them, Fig. 6. Don overdo your application! It's better t gradually build up the color to the de sired level. White mixed with ligh gray gives a good salt effect, and or ange is the obvious choice for rust. T keep the brushed-on pastels in place, ply a light overspray of Micro Coat lat. If you have overdone an area, ap-y more flat to tone it down.

More simple improvements. Do the st of the construction according to the t instructions, although we'll make a w improvements along the way. The rrets on Japanese light cruisers were ted with blast bags, and these can be ade from white glue. Begin by brush-g a little glue into the opening be-een the gun barrel and the splinter ield, then gradually build up the bag, ig. 7, checking the box art for the ap-ropriate size. After the glue has dried, int the bags white (or another appro-iate color).

The rear of this kit's shelter deck eeded putty to seal a seam and to ild up sink marks. The shelter deck d bridge should lie flat when they're ounted. Check this alignment before uing, and sand the bottoms of these eces if necessary. Also check the eight of structures, such as the shelter ck, with the height of the decks they ill be joined to — there should be no ep up or down. Minor seams can be led with white glue and a fine brush, llowed by a paint touch-up.

Be sure to sand out as many glue ams as you can during construction. ttention to basic construction is im-rtant in ship modeling, too.

Although the lifeboat interior detail that is provided in this kit is nicely done, the same isn't always true with other waterline kits. The easiest way to hide poor lifeboat interiors is to put covers on them (standard equipment on Japanese vessels, anyway). I fill the boats with putty, Fig. 8. Be sure to use a putty that doesn't shrink much when applied in thick layers. My favorite filler for all puttying jobs is Duratite Surfacing Putty. After the putty dries, sand it smooth and paint the covers white, Fig. 9.

The tops of the fore and aft masts and flagstaffs should be replaced, since these pieces are too thick and out of scale. Also, yards and spars don't grow out of masts — they are attached to them, Fig. 10. I make replacement pieces by stretching clear plastic sprue (it's stiffer and less likely to change shape than colored sprue).

If you decide to use the window stickers given with many waterline kits, fasten the ends with a little white glue (because they tend to lift off). On the *Kuma*, these observation windows were covered with white canvas when not in use, so they can be painted on the model. The Japanese used lots of white canvas on their vessels, as shown on the kit box art. I prefer Polly S white for canvas — the fine brush marks give the effect of wind wrinkling the canvas.

The fit of the tripod masts and the searchlight platforms on the *Kuma* need to be carefully reworked, as on most ship kits. Take your time and do as much dry-fitting as you can before gluing them in place. If there are any gaps left, fill them with white glue, Fig. 12. Check the mast alignment from the front and side and make adjustments as the glue sets. Nothing looks worse than leaning masts.

Final weathering. After all of the kit parts have been painted and glued in place, final weathering can begin. Treat forward deck structures such as the turrets, base of the bridge, and structures along the outer sides of the deck with pastels to achieve the effects of salt spray. The mine rails and bilge vents can be given a dusting of rust pastel to show corrosion. When you're happy with the weathering, overspray the entire model with clear flat, and you're done — and ready for your *second* waterline ship kit! **FSM**

SOURCES

● Chain: Campbell Scale Models, available from Wm. Walthers Inc., P.O. Box 18676, Milwaukee, WI 53218
● Duratite Surfacing Putty: DAP Inc., Dayton, OH 45401
● Flex-i-file: Creations Unlimited, 2939 Montreat Drive N.E., Grand Rapids, MI 49505.

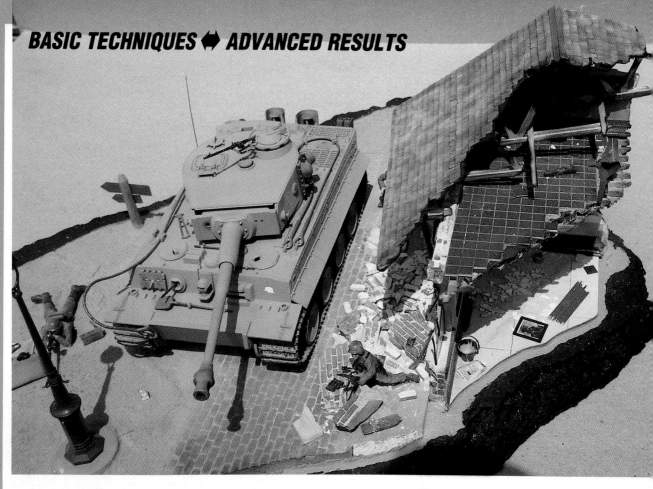

Titled "Delaying action," Jack's diorama depicts three soldiers and a tank next to a bombed-out house.

Structures and groundwork for your first diorama

Down-to-earth methods

BY JACK SMITH

FOR THE PAST several years I modeled mostly aircraft. Then I tried a few tanks and figures, and a whole new world of modeling and techniques opened up. There was one area I still wanted to try: an armor diorama with buildings.

I thought through the story and setting for my 1/35 scale diorama and tried to keep it simple. Anyone can plan a grandiose layout and then get bogged down in the execution. It's sufficient to have just enough background material to set a mood and just enough military equipment to tell a story.

Following this theme I decided on one bombed-out building and located it at the end of a street, eliminating the need for a large scene. My story is a

rear guard delaying action by three German soldiers and a Tiger tank.

How big a base? I arranged my tank and unassembled building on a table top in what I considered a reasonable layout. I then measured the base required and cut an irregular-shaped base from 1"-thick plastic foam insulation.

I brushed lacquer thinner sparingly along the edge with a ½"-wide brush to seal the cut edge. The thinner dissolves the foam, so practice on scrap first.

Building. Now I was ready to tackle my first structure, a Kurton bombed-out building (Kurton Products is no longer in business, but Verlinden Productions offers similar structures). First I read the instructions to familiarize myself with the product and see if any special techniques were required. The worst aspect of the job was

painting the bricks, which I did one a time. It took several nights to fini this step. When paint got on the mor joints I simply ran a point down t groove to scrape the paint off, Fig. 1.

The interior took considerable pl ning. What kind of floors, walls, a trim to use? The kit was made of u fired ceramic clay, similar to plaster, the easiest method was to paint t walls and scribe cracks and bullet ho in the surface, Fig. 2.

For the floor on the first level I us marble-finished Masonite scribed i square sections with a few cracks, F 2. I made the second floor from wo with floor joists and lathing for t first-story ceiling. The constructi was a mixture of balsa strips and ha wood sheets with planked and lath f ishes cut into them, Fig. 3. The plank

Fig. 1. Kurton products provided the basic bombed-out building; ack provided the paint and time to finish it.

Fig. 2. The bare kit interior has been detailed with a Masonite floor, baseboard, and window sills.

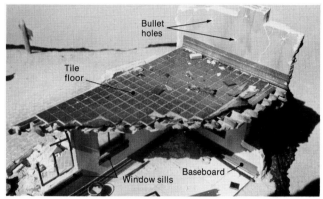

Fig. 3. The second story was made like the real thing. Balsa and rdwood sheets were used to make the floor.

Fig. 4. Plastic sheet painted to resemble tile was added as the second-story floor. The baseboard is dollhouse material.

bfloor was topped with a tile surface. e tiles are simulated by an Ever-een plastic ¼″ scale (1/48) tile sheet, g. 4. The baseboard, window sill, and her wood trim were sections from im produced by Northeastern Scale odels Inc. for dollhouses.

Go ahead and finish extra pieces of im and break them up for use as de-is. The pieces do not have to match rticular building sections.

Ceiling. The first-floor plaster ceil-g was difficult to make, because wet aster will warp wood. I had to pre-rm the plaster, then attach it to the th work. I mixed plaster in a small sh and spread it over a sheet of thick vergreen plastic sheet to a depth of out ¹/₃₂″ with an old credit card used a spreader. When the plastic was wed carefully, the plaster lifted off in single smooth sheet. I glued this eet to the ceiling lath and trimmed ong the straight sides with a razor ade. Where the construction is bro-n and ragged, I carefully broke off all sections, Fig. 5. Careful pressure

with your fingertips will create realis-tic cracks.

Don't worry if pieces fall off, just glue them back on. I then mixed a spoonful of plaster (very thin) and used this to brush a thin coat over the exposed lath.

Sidewalk. I made the sidewalk from a scrap piece of construction plaster-board. By wetting the paper facing on the plasterboard, it can easily be stripped off. I worked slowly, as the plasterboard is easily broken when it's wet. If it does break, save the pieces and reassemble them when they dry. This will produce a cracked sidewalk adjoining the building — added real-ism, Fig. 6.

I used two sections of Kurton cobble-stone for my street. These sections were cast from the same material used in the buildings and were easy to carve. I cut out several stones at the end of the street; this looked more realistic than a straight edge, Fig. 6.

Photos and small details. Taking photos for the article at this point in the construction helped improve my

additional detail work. I spotted things in the photos that didn't look right or were missing.

I studied my references again and made a list of small details to include. Some things worth considering were lamp posts, fences, posters, abandoned equipment, oil drums, trees, and rub-ble. A word of caution: Don't overdo the scene with too much stuff.

I sprayed the perimeter of the base with flat black enamel, then dry-fit the major components of the diorama on the base. When I was satisfied with the positions, I glued down the ruined building, sidewalk, and street. I used super glue, spraying liberally with "Hot Shot" accelerator to keep the glue from eating into the plastic foam.

Adding a little model mud. I used dirt dug from my front yard and sifted through a tea strainer. The coarse mat-ter was kept separate to sprinkle on top later. I mixed the dirt with water and Elmer's Glue-All — the right consist-ency is thin enough to spread easily with a butter knife. I worked the model

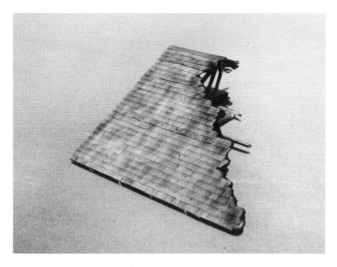

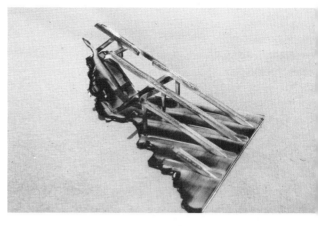

Figs. 11 and 12. The roof was weathered using a cigarette lighter to singe the edges.

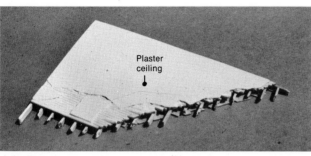

Fig. 5. The first-floor ceiling is a thin layer of plaster glued to the underside of the second-story floor. Note how cracking and pieces create a realistic effect.

Fig. 8 CEILING TRUSS PLAN

mud up to the edge of the building and the street, keeping it away from the items covering the rest of the base. While the mud was still wet, I made track and tread marks where traffic would have moved, Fig. 7. I also added Static Grass while the mud was still wet and sprinkled on pebbles from the strained dirt. I let this dry for a couple days, then mixed more model mud and brushed it into the cracks.

Adding the details. Posts were set by boring a hole in the dirt and using white glue to hold them in place. I brushed model mud around the base to fill any voids. I used burning strips of wood to blacken the walls and burn the edges of the broken structure. Charcoal pastels were also used to dirty up the building. Charcoal ash from my barbecue grill was dusted inside the building and on the sidewalk to simulate wood ashes. Individual Kurton bricks were brushed with plaster to simulate mortar on the exposed mating surfaces, dirtied up a bit, and then spread around the building. I selected a shade of charcoal pastel that matched the dirt and dusted it over the street, then brushed it off, leaving some in the grooves, Fig. 7.

Roof. To tell the truth the roof was an afterthought. The diorama was basically complete, but while looking at the photos one night, I decided it didn't look quite finished. I looked in my books and saw a lot of roofs caved in and resting on the second floor, so I decided to add one myself.

First, I drew a truss design on paper, Fig. 8. Then, I built two complete units from balsa wood which were cut into four sections of progressively longer lengths. These were jigged up on a flat surface and balsa roof planks glued in place, Figs. 9 and 10. Black paper was glued over the planking to simulate tar paper and Kappler wooden shingles (a model railroad item) were installed. I then carefully burned the complete structure using a cigarette lighter, Figs. 11 and 12. The roof was finally glued in place using Elmer's Glue-All.

I hope this article will encourage you to try a diorama of your own. It isn't difficult, but it will take planning and patience. Don't let the work of people

Fig. 6. Jack made the sidewalk from plasterboard with its paper backing removed; the street is Kurton cobblestone.

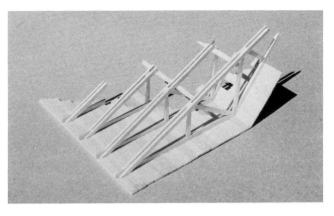

g. 9. Raising the roof — or part of it, anyway. Balsa planks are ued to the roof truss.

Fig. 10. Here's a better view of the roof truss. When you're satisfied with this assembly, cover the roof with black paper.

ke Sheperd Paine intimidate you; ather, use it as an inspiration to jump a and get your feet wet. Remember, 's fun, and you don't have to win any rophies. If it looks good to you, then it ooks good enough — period! **FSM**

SOURCES

Styrene sheet, rod, tubing, and pat-rned styrene: Evergreen Scale Mod-ls, 12808 N. E. 125th Way, Kirkland, VA 98034

Styrene structural forms, sheet, rod, ubing, and patterned styrene: Plas-ruct, 1020 S. Wallace Place, City of In-ustry, CA 91748

Diorama building materials and ac-essories: Dutton Enterprises, P. O. Box 77, Oakhurst, CA 93644

Diorama building materials and ac-essories: VLS Products, Lone Star In-ustrial Park, 811 Lone Star Drive, 'Fallon, MO 63366

Scale lumber: Kappler Mill & Lum-er Co., 1760 Monrovia, A-15, Costa Iesa, CA 92627

Dollhouse parts: Northeastern Scale Iodels, 99 Cross St., P.O. Box 727, Me-nuen, MA 01844

Tread marks

Fig. 7. You can model tread marks while the groundwork is still wet. Add rubble, then dust the scene with charcoal ash and powdered pastels.

Stretched sprue rivets, hinges, and communication antenna improved this 1/35 scale SdKfz 165 Hummel. Photos by the authors.

BASIC TECHNIQUES ◆ ADVANCED RESULTS

The art of stretching sprue

One of the first and most important detailing techniques to learn

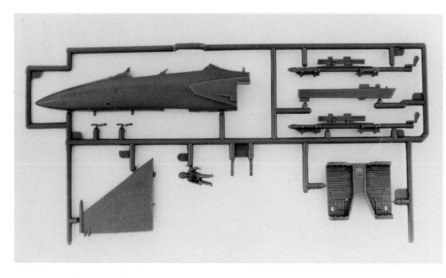

Fig. 1. Sprue is the plastic that holds the kit parts.

**BY BOB DYE
AND MICHAEL MACKOWSKI**

WHEN YOU'RE READY to venture beyond kit instructions to conversions and scratchbuilding, one of the first and most useful detailing techniques you'll learn is how to stretch sprue. Stretched sprue has dozens of uses and it's easy to make. We'll cover some of these uses and show you how to stretch sprue.

What is sprue? Sprue is the plastic runner that holds the parts in an injection-molded plastic kit, Fig. 1. Molten plastic is forced through channels to the mold cavities that form the kit parts. When the plastic cools, the parts and their attached sprues are pushed out of the mold.

Usually sprue is round, but sometimes

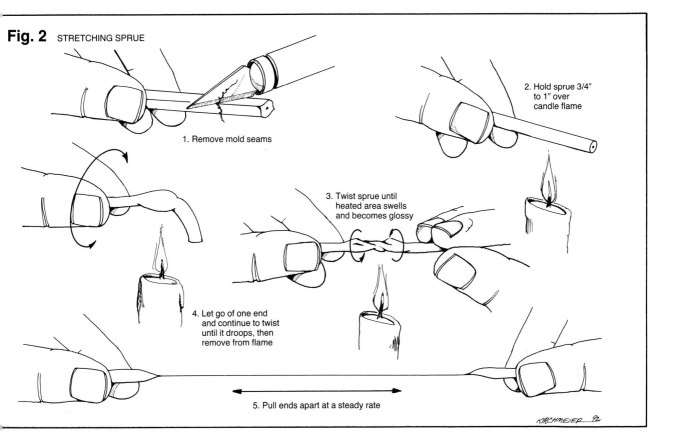

Fig. 2 STRETCHING SPRUE

1. Remove mold seams

2. Hold sprue 3/4″ to 1″ over candle flame

3. Twist sprue until heated area swells and becomes glossy

4. Let go of one end and continue to twist until it droops, then remove from flame

5. Pull ends apart at a steady rate

KIRCHMEIER 9z

is half round, square, or hexagonal in cross section. Sprue will retain its original shape even after you stretch it. If sprue is asymmetrical due to mismatched molds, stretched sprue will also be asymmetrical. If sprue is hexagonal, the stretched sprue will be hexagonal, and so forth.

Because plastic sprue comes in different colors, you may not have to paint after stretching it. Clear canopy sprue and the transparent red from taillights can make small light lenses. Stiff plastic (as used by Tamiya) produces sturdy stretched sprue, while more pliable soft plastic (like Italeri's) can be stretched thin. The rubbery material used for tank treads can make bendable stretched sprue.

Candles in the wind. Candles are the best heat source for stretching sprue because they generate just the right amount of heat for the job. Short, thick candles provide a stable flame useful for fine control when heating sprue. Thin, tall candles have a hotter, unstable flame.

Once you light the candle, wait for the flame and its temperature to stabilize. Tall, thin candles stabilize in less than 30 seconds, while short, fat candles take two or three minutes. Place the candle where breezes and drafts won't disturb the flame.

It's easy. Choose straight sprue without part stubs. Sand off mold parting lines to produce a smooth, constant cross section. Don't cut the sprue too short: It will be hard to handle, and you could fry your fingers. A 4″-long section is just right. Now you're ready to stretch.

Hold the middle of the sprue about 3/4″ to 1″ over the flame, Fig. 2. If you get too close to the flame, you'll burn the sprue or melt it in two. Get too far from the flame and you will have to take longer to heat the sprue. Avoid igniting the plastic: The fumes from burning styrene aren't good for you.

With both hands, twirl the sprue between your fingers to heat it evenly. When the sprue swells and becomes shiny, it's nearly ready to stretch. You also know the sprue is softening when you no longer feel a "connection" between your right and left hands. At this point, release one hand and continue to twirl the sprue with the other hand until the free end droops over. Now remove the sprue from the flame; continue to twirl.

Grab the loose end and begin to pull the ends apart. See how the hot plastic "strings" as you pull the sprue apart? That's what you want: stretched sprue! Pull the ends apart rapidly so you get two or three inches of stretched sprue, then slow down — but continue to pull. Once you get the hang of it, you can establish the diameter of the stretched sprue during the initial pull. Then slowly but steadily stretch the sprue, maintaining the same diameter as you

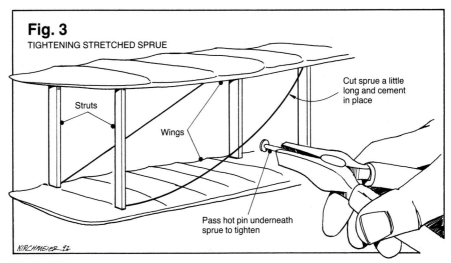

Fig. 3
TIGHTENING STRETCHED SPRUE

Cut sprue a little long and cement in place

Struts

Wings

Pass hot pin underneath sprue to tighten

KIRCHMEIER 9z

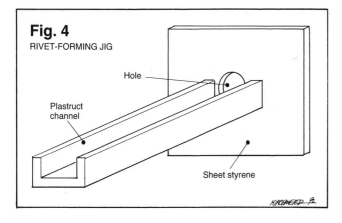

Fig. 4
RIVET-FORMING JIG

Hole

Plastruct channel

Sheet styrene

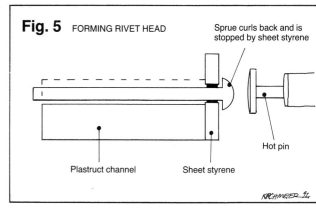

Fig. 5   FORMING RIVET HEAD

Sprue curls back and is stopped by sheet styrene

Hot pin

Plastruct channel

Sheet styrene

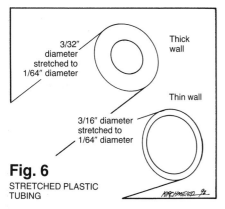

3/32" diameter stretched to 1/64" diameter

Thick wall

Thin wall

3/16" diameter stretched to 1/64" diameter

Fig. 6
STRETCHED PLASTIC TUBING

USES FOR STRETCHED SPRUE		
Wheel spokes	Rivets	Axles
Radio antennas	Marker lights	Aircraft rigging
Gun barrels	Cigarettes	Cross-hair sights
Rod antennas	Canopy hinges	Door and hatch hinges
Pitot tubes	Ammunition	Panel reinforcements
Landing gear struts	Ladders	Hydraulic cylinders
Instrument panel switches	Bomb fuses	Spot applicator for super glue

TROUBLESHOOTING STRETCHED SPRUE

Sometimes stretching sprue doesn't go smoothly. Here are some of the more common problems and their solutions:

● *Sprue breaks when stretching.*
You're pulling too quickly. Slow down.

● *Sprue varies in diameter along length.*
You are probably pulling unevenly. Practice a steady pull. Inhale before pulling, and exhale while pulling, or pull after exhaling (hold your breath). Believe it or not, your heartbeat produces little jumps as you pull the sprue. You should be relaxed.

● *Sprue is bowed.*
This develops from uneven cooling of the plastic. Make sure the sprue is fully and evenly heated before stretching, and make sure you let it cool properly.

● *Asymmetric cross section.*
The two usual causes of this are a cross section that's already assymetric or prominent mold seams. It could also be caused by squeezing the molten sprue out of round before or during the stretching process. Don't try to stretch a short length of sprue. Be sure you have enough hard sprue on either side of the molten section to maintain a round cross section. This also keeps you from grabbing sprue that's too hot to handle.

We don't recommend using pliers or other instruments to hold the plastic. You don't need a gorilla's grip on the sprue. It's more important to feel the sprue as it heats and stretches.

go. For thick stretched sprue, wait a few seconds as you continue to twirl, allowing the plastic to cool slightly.

The plastic has been cooling down ever since you removed the sprue from the flame. As you continue to pull, the cooling sprue becomes less elastic. Eventually you won't be able to stretch it any farther. Since thin stretched sprue has to be pulled rapidly, you can easily pull more than three feet before the sprue cools.

When you feel resistance, it's time to slow down. Exert just enough outward pressure to hold the stretched sprue taut for a few seconds as it cools. This keeps the sprue from bowing or warping.

Rigging and antennas. Some of the more common uses for stretched sprue are listed in Table 1. It's long been used for rigging wires on biplanes and ship models and for antenna wires on aircraft and armor.

When spanning an area with thin stretched sprue, cut each piece 1/16" to 1/8" longer than needed and attach both ends, Fig. 3. Passing a hot pin near the sprue can make it taut. With pliers, hold a small sewing pin in a candle flame until the pin is red hot. The heat causes the sprue to shrink slightly, eliminating the slack. A better heating instrument (but one more difficult to find) is punk — composition sticks used for lighting fireworks. Punk burns slowly, similar to incense. Simply pass the lit punk underneath the sagging sprue and watch the sprue tighten.

Rivets, fake and functional. You ca use stretched sprue to simulate rive or even to make them function as re rivets. Start by stretching round spr to the approximate thickness you nee for the rivet shank.

Try to produce a single long strand stretched sprue with a constant diam ter throughout. The diameter of t shank is one factor that determines t diameter of the finished rivet head. C off the ends and you're ready for t next step.

A simple jig for forming rivet hea can be made from a one-inch-squa piece of .040"-thick sheet styrene. Y need thick plastic to keep the riv head perpendicular to the shank, Fi 4. In the middle of the square, drill small hole slightly larger than the d ameter of the stretched sprue you'll u for the rivets. I cemented a 4"-lo piece of Plastruct channel to the ba of my jig to help keep the stretche sprue perpendicular to the hole.

Insert the stretched sprue in the ho in the jig until the sprue protrud through the other side. The length the protruding sprue determines t size of the finished rivet head.

Now heat the head of a straight pin the candle flame. When the pin is r hot, place the head next to (but n touching) the protruding rivet shan The hot pin makes the sprue curl ba on itself; the curling stops when t sprue reaches the styrene square. Allo the sprue to cool for a few seconds, pu

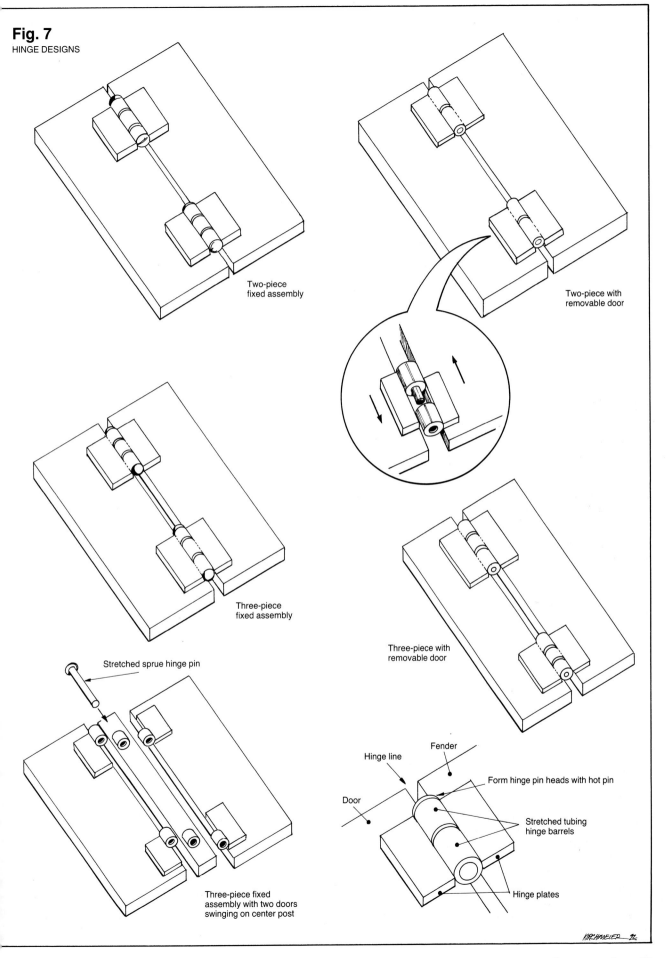

Fig. 7
HINGE DESIGNS

Two-piece
fixed assembly

Two-piece with
removable door

Three-piece
fixed assembly

Three-piece with
removable door

Stretched sprue hinge pin

Three-piece fixed
assembly with two doors
swinging on center post

Hinge line

Fender

Door

Form hinge pin heads with hot pin

Stretched tubing
hinge barrels

Hinge plates

KIRCHMEIER 92

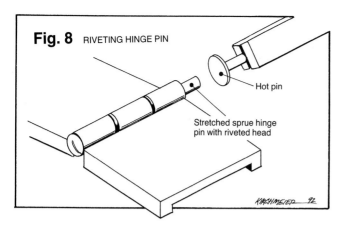

Fig. 8 RIVETING HINGE PIN

Hot pin

Stretched sprue hinge pin with riveted head

KIRCHMEIER 92

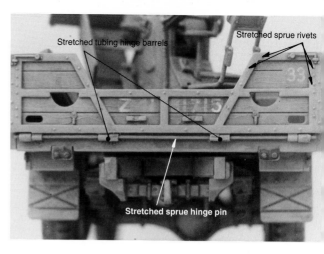

Stretched tubing hinge barrels

Stretched sprue rivets

Stretched sprue hinge pin

Fig. 9. The tailgate on this 1/35 scale model of a captured Britis 15 cwt truck swings on a hinge of stretched tube and sprue. Als note the sprue rivets on the tailgate frame.

Two-piece working hinges

Fig. 10. A closeup of the same truck as in Fig. 9, showing the working two-piece door hinges.

Three-piece hinges on center post

Fig. 11. This 1/35 scale Tamiya Kubelwagen features workin three-piece hinges mounted to a center post.

it out of the jig, and cut off the rivet head with as long a shank as you need, Fig. 5.

Insert the finished rivets in small holes drilled in the model. Cement the rivets in place from the back or inside if you can. With practice, you could form a head on the other end of the shank using the hot pin method. Imagine armor plates attached to brackets with miniature rivets that work just like the original's!

Hinges. If solid styrene sprue can be stretched, why not styrene tube? It works! Thin stretched styrene tube has many uses: gun barrels, sighting tubes, and pitot tubes, to name a few. And stretching tube opens a door on . . . opening doors. You can make working hinges from stretched tubing and stretched sprue.

Evergreen Scale Models makes styrene tube in many sizes. Follow the technique used for stretching sprue, but don't stretch the tube so thin it will be unusable. While the outside and inside diameters of the different sizes vary, the wall thickness of Evergreen tubing is nearly consistent in all sizes. When stretched, the diameter and wall thickness are reduced. However, the wall thickness of $3/16''$ (outside diame-

ter) tubing when stretched to $1/64''$ (o.d.) is thinner than the wall thickness of $3/32''$ stretched to $1/64''$. If the outside diameter is the same and the wall thickness is different, the inside diameter must be different, too, Fig. 6. Thinner walls are more fragile, but they will accept thicker hinge pins made from stretched sprue.

Cutting stretched tubing is tricky; scissors or a dull blade will crush the fragile tubing. Instead, draw a sharp blade (preferably a single-edge razor blade) lightly across the tube. Use the notch made by the first pass to realign the blade for the next pass. A brand new blade will give you clean cuts.

Figure 7 shows five different hinge designs: two-part fixed; two-part removable; three-part fixed; three-part removable; and three-part with center jamb. All these designs allow the door, lid, or hatch to swing on miniature stretched-sprue hinge pins.

Again, a heated pin produces the rivet head on the hinge pin. For fixed pins with heads on both ends, cut the shank a little longer than necessary, then form the head after the pin is installed in the hinge, Fig. 8. Be careful: Heating the sprue too much will make

it squeeze the hinge elements, causing bind. Try placing a strip of paper or strand of hair between any of the ele ments before you form the second head Then remove the paper or hair. This wi keep the hinge loose enough to operate.

Attaching hinges. You can't attac hinges to the model with liquid solven cements or standard thin super glue Capillary action will weld the element together better than rust does on a rea hinge. Use a thick, fast-setting cement such as a gap-filling super glue.

Since such hinges usually require out side hinge plates, use small plates cu from thin sheet styrene to position th hinges quickly. A spot of glue will attac each barrel of the hinge to the appropri ate part. It takes work, but the result are worth it. Just take a look at th working hinges in Figs. 9, 10, and 11.

All stretched out. With practice an some imagination, you'll find hundred of uses for stretched sprue. You'll als discover that working with stretche sprue is not a mystical art. **FSM**

SOURCE

● Sheet, tube, and rod styrene: Ever green Scale Models, 12808 N. E. 125t Way, Kirkland, WA 98034

iny red, green, and amber lenses are perfect for World War wo ID lights found on some fighter aircraft. The lenses come in wide variety of sizes and colors. FSM photo: Paul Boyer

Realistic light lenses for models

mprove your headlights, anding lights, spotlights, taillights . . .

BY JIM STEEL

[WAS BROWSING in the model railroad section of a hobby shop and discovered a wide variety of tiny lenses, erfect for detailing my models. They're produced by M. V. Products, and are available from hobby shops and Wm. K. Walthers Inc., P. O. Box 18676, Milwaukee, WI 53218. Each s a glass-like clear polymer lens with a silvered rear face.

M. V. Products' lenses aren't lights, but large lenses can e modified by drilling holes in the back and inserting mall grain-of-wheat bulbs. Even if you don't want to light hem, a hole drilled from the back gives the impression of a ulb inside the lens. The largest lens available is ½″ in di- ameter while the smallest is .052″ diameter. Many of the izes are also available in red, green, amber, and blue. The able gives the sizes, colors, and stock numbers. In addition o those listed, M. V. Products also packages small assort- nents for use on specific model railroad locomotives.

Many uses. The lenses can be used to enhance just about very type of model. Car modelers can use the larger sizes or headlights and some of the red lenses are good for tail- ights. Blue lenses can be used for emergency vehicles such s police cars and fire equipment. Armor modelers will like hem for headlights, taillights, spotlights, optical sights, angefinders, and field glass lenses. For aircraft models, the lear lenses are perfect for landing and taxi lights, while he red and green can be used for position lights. The red, green, and amber ID lights on some U. S. fighters of World War Two can be made easily. Clear lenses also make perfect nfrared seeker lenses for Sidewinder and Falcon missiles!

Mounting lenses. It's simple to attach the lenses. The ta- ole provides matching drill sizes that can be used to coun- ersink mounts for the lenses. A drill press makes this job asier. Simply drill a depression in the plastic or metal where you want to mount the lens. Attach the lens with su- oer glue, epoxy, or white glue — it's made of a substance hat is impervious to most solvent cements and thinners. If you paint over or tint a lens, cleaning with thinner houldn't damage it.

With a little more imagination, you can probably find lozens of other uses for these tiny lenses. **FSM**

BASIC TECHNIQUES ⬥ ADVANCED RESULTS

DRILL SIZE	DIAMETER INCH MILLIMETER	M. V. PRODUCTS STOCK NUMBERS				
		Clear	Red	Green	Amber	Blue
55	.052″, 1.32 mm	LS 300	LS 301	LS 302	LS 303	LS 506
52	.063″, 1.62 mm	LS 22	LS 220	LS 221	LS 222	LS 507
49	.073″, 1.85 mm	LS 26	LS 103			
47	.078″, 1.99 mm	LS 25	LS 24			
45	.082″, 2.08 mm	LS 28	LS 28			
44	.086″, 2.18 mm	LS 20	LS 200	LS 201	LS 202	LS 508
41	.096″, 2.43 mm	L 409	L 410	L 411	L 412	
38	.101″, 2.58 mm	LS 29	LS 30		LS 31	LS 32
32	.116″, 2.94 mm	L 116	L 117			
30	.128″, 3.26 mm	L 128	L 129		L 130	L 131
29	.136″, 3.45 mm	L 136	L 137		L 138	L 139
25	.149″, 3.79 mm	L 149	L 150			
21	.159″, 4.03 mm	L 159	L 160			
19	.166″, 4.21 mm	L 166	L 167		L 168	L 169
17	.173″, 4.39 mm	L 173	L 174			
15	.180″, 4.57 mm	L 180	L 181		L 182	L 183
13	.185″, 4.69 mm	L 185				
10	.193″, 4.91 mm	L 193				
8	.199″, 5.08 mm	L 199	L 198		L 197	
6	.204″, 5.18 mm	L 204				
4	.209″, 5.30 mm	L 209	L 210	L 211	L 212	
2	.221″, 5.61 mm	L 218	L 216		L 217	
1	.228″, 5.79 mm	L 228	L 229		L 230	L 231
15/64″	.234″, 5.94 mm	L 401				
1/4″	.250″, 6.35 mm	L 248				
17/64″	.265″, 6.73 mm	L 402				
9/32″	.281″, 7.13 mm	L 403	L 414		L 415	
19/64″	.296″, 7.51 mm	L 404				
5/16″	.312″, 7.92 mm	L 400				
21/64″	.328″, 8.33 mm	L 405				
11/32″	.343″, 8.71 mm	L 406				
23/64″	.359″, 9.11 mm	L 407				
3/8″	.375″, 9.57 mm	L 408				
1/2″	.500″, 12.7 mm	L 413				

Details make the difference

Basic add-ons that make your car or truck model unique

Roy's MPC '88 Silverado pickup in sunshine yellow shows the detailing treatment described in this article. Note the tinted bug deflector on the hood.

BY ROY SORENSON

EVEN THE SIMPLEST car models can become standouts if you add a few small details. And thanks to today's technology and the many products from cottage industries at our disposal, adding extra details is easier than it used to be.

The kit I chose for my detail lesson is MPC's '88 Silverado pickup (kit No. 6096). This kit is clean, well detailed, and easy to assemble — perfect for beginners or experts. Follow along as we add those little details that count.

Paint stand. Before you paint your car model, cement all the parts to the body that will be painted the same color as the body. Of course, if you want the hood, trunk, or doors to open, don't cement them now! Attaching as many parts as you can will allow the paint to cover many glue spots and seams

Make a paint stand like mine from a 1"-diameter pipe welded to a steel plate, Fig. 1. Attach the car model body to the pipe and the hood and fire wall to the steel plate with double-sided tape. By elevating the body you can spray it from all directions.

A better front end. To improve the appearance of the chrome-plated grille Fig. 2, flow flat black paint into the re

Fig. 1. A paint stand made from a steel plate and pipe makes painting car bodies a lot easier.

Fig. 2. Flat black paint inside the recesses of the grille adds a touch of realism.

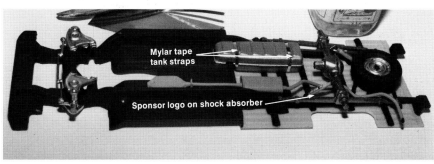
Mylar tape tank straps

Sponsor logo on shock absorber

Fig. 3. Roy uses a paper punch to make small disks of fine brass mesh for the air cleaner.

Fig. 6. The sponsor decals that come with many car kits can be used to label the performance accessories such as shock absorbers and oil filters. Chromed Mylar tape can improve the gas tank straps.

Fig. 4. Flat white paint, a fine brush, and a steady hand are all you need to finish the raised letters on tires. Tire logos can be found on aftermarket decals, too.

esses. Before it dries completely, use a soft cloth to carefully rub off any paint that gets on the raised grille.

Paint the turn signal lights with clear yellow or clear amber acrylic paint. You can make a bug deflector from clear acetate and color it with clear-tint acrylics. Attach the acetate with Bare-Metal Foil, a self-adhesive, thin aluminum foil that is also ideal for chrome trim.

Filtering techniques. I use LMG Enterprises brass screen for filters on the

air cleaner. The brass screen is fine, and it's easy to cut perfect circles with a hole punch, Fig. 3. As an added touch, I applied a Fram sponsor decal from another kit to the oil filter.

Nice wheels. As with the grille, I used flat black paint in the recesses of the chrome wheels. The white lettering on the tires can either be hand painted or made from a decal, Fig. 4. Fred Cady Design's decal sheet No. 183 has Goodyear Eagle and Firestone Balloon logos, along with dashboard gauge faces.

Interior insight. Paint buildup on the dashboard can make it hard to detail. To keep the spray paint off, I used Microscale's Micro Mask, Fig. 5. This is a liquid masking agent you apply with a brush. When it's dry, you paint, then remove the mask with tweezers. Detail the gauges with black, white, and red paint and a fine brush.

Underside improvements. I improved the gas tank straps with thin strips of chrome Mylar tape, Fig. 6. Sponsor decals from a stock-car kit were used on the shock absorbers. To get decals to conform to the curved surfaces of the shocks, I used a decal solvent. Solvent softens the decals and allows them to bend around curves.

That personal touch. Adding miniature personalized license plates to your

car models is easier than it used to be, thanks to a few small manufacturers, Fig. 7. The frames are photoetched metal from Detail Masters, the "Chevy" and "Yu lose" plates with custom frames are also photoetched products from Tyresmoke Industries, and the letter decal sheet comes from California Decals.

I hope you can use some of these tips to improve your car and truck models. Little details such as these can set your model apart. **FSM**

SOURCES

● Bare-Metal Foil: Bare-Metal Foil & Hobby Co., P. O. Box 82, Farmington, MI 48024

● Automobile decals: Fred Cady Design, P. O. Box 576, Mount Prospect, IL 60056

● License plate decals: California Decals, P. O. Box 7101, Oakland, CA 94601

● License plate frames: Detail Masters, 8411 Bayou Pine, No. A3, Houston, TX 77040

● Brass screen: LMG Enterprises, 1627 South 26th Street, Sheboygan, WI 53081

● License plates: Tyresmoke Industries, available from Model Storehouse, 8580 Gaines Avenue, Orangevale, CA 95662

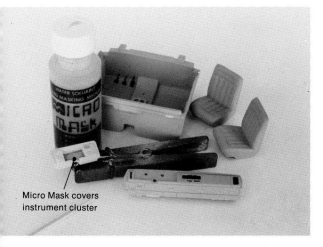
Micro Mask covers instrument cluster

Fig. 5. Liquid maskers such as Micro Mask can be used to keep paint from covering the details on the instrument cluster.

Fig. 7. Many cottage-industry products can add that personal touch to your car model. License plates are available in many forms.

Ten ways to improve your 1/24 scale NASCAR racer model

Taking the easy way to the best results

Superdetailing can work wonders! Check out this spoiler made from a soda can.

...per detail doesn't have to mean a long, exhausting job.

BY TIM BONGARD

SCRATCHBUILDING or superdetailing models sometimes seems overwhelmingly complicated. But if you'll regard each detail as a simple improvement, a miniature model you're adding to the basic kit, you'll find your project more manageable — and fun!

Here are 10 ways to improve a NASCAR chassis in less than an hour per step. (You may need to practice.) And because most racing rules on safety equipment and other devices are standardized, these techniques are relevant to many other models, from karts to dragsters.

Finding detailing parts can be difficult. If they are unavailable at your favorite hobby shop, mail order or swap meets are alternatives. And keep an open mind about the original purpose of each part: We'll use a few items not intended for model cars. But they provide the right look.

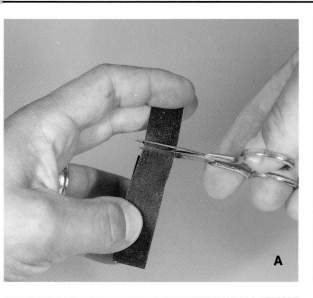

A

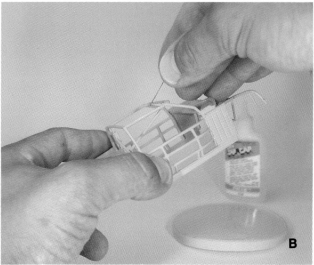

B

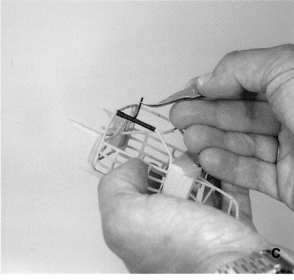

C

Step 1. Roll cage padding. This is a prominent detail on any racer. I use black electrical friction tape, the tarlike forerunner of vinyl electrical tape. You can still find it at hardware stores and home centers.

Start by building your roll cage assembly and painting it the appropriate color for your model. Cut the friction tape to the desired length with scissors (**A**). Using a pin or a sewing needle, apply a drop of gap-filling super glue to the tape for extra adhesion (**B**). Then apply the tape to the roll cage and wrap it around the tube. When the tape almost encircles the tube, apply another thin bead of glue to the tape. If you rub lightly on the seam where the tape ends, the seam will nearly disappear.

Vinyl electrical tape fastens most padding on the real cars. To duplicate this you'll use — vinyl electrical tape. Lay a piece of vinyl tape on glass. With a straightedge and a hobby knife, cut the tape into strips about 1 mm wide. Using tweezers or prongs, wrap these thin strips around the friction tape (**C**). Anchor both ends by applying super glue as described above. If the fabric tape's texture appears rough, simply smooth it.

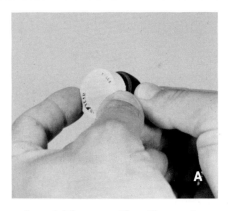

Step 2. Tire stenciling. Few real racing tires carry raised white lettering. Instead, brand markings are stenciled on the sidewall, often roughly.

Replicas & Miniatures' stencil kit for Monogram 1/24 scale cars, No. RM-14A, includes a photoetched brass stencil with a plastic fixture to hold the tire during painting. Replicas' instructions also list paints that adhere well to vinyl rubber tires.

Begin by sanding each tire with open-coat sandpaper, 120 grit on the tread and 220 grit on the raised letters. (Brisk rubbing with denim will restore the sidewall's luster.) Next slide the tire into the stencil (**A**), and spray it with a fast-drying paint such as Floquil white figure primer or Reefer White railroad paint (**B**). To avoid smearing, let the tire dry before removing it from the stencil.

Polly S also works here, but avoid using the typical hobby enamels: They just won't dry on the tires.

Step 3. Rear spoiler. The rear spoilers on injection-molded racer kits usually look thick. Make an inexpensive, easy-to-work-with, and easy-to-find replacement with aluminum from a soda can. You can cut it with scissors or a hobby knife, bend it with your fingers, and smooth it with fine sandpaper or steel wool. Polishing with Du Pont No. 7 Polishing Compound produces a brilliant, natural-metal look.

Using the original part as a template (**A**), trace the shape with a pin or a pencil. Cut the tracing with sharp scissors, then polish the rough edges with 000C steel wool or 400-grit sandpaper. To paint the spoiler, mask its back half (**B**), and spray it with Testor's Flat Black. Glue metal parts with a gap-filling super glue — or 5-minute epoxy for easy removal in case of blunders. Use extra hardener in the epoxy for a faster set. If you find soda-can aluminum too thin, try aluminum roof flashing — or Canadian cans, which use heavier-gauge aluminum.

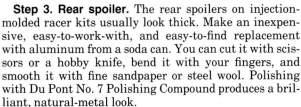

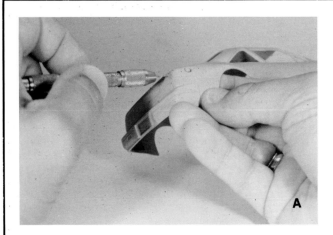

Step 4. Fuel overflow pipe. Most racer kits omit the fuel overflow pipe, which vents extra fuel and vapors on most stock cars.

To add an overflow pipe, drill a 1/16″ hole in the back end of the body shell (**A**). With a round file, open a slight hole for a short aluminum tube. Check whether your prototype's tube is natural-metal or matches the body; wait until you've painted to add a natural-metal tube. Either way, drill and size the hole before painting or priming.

Secure the tube with a drop of super glue applied from inside the body shell, then ream the tube with a round jeweler's file for a realistic thin look. If your trunk opens, connect the overflow tube to the fuel cell with a clear neoprene tube; attach it to the smaller of the two pickups atop the cell. Even in recent AMT kits, which supply the pipes, this approach will enhance your details.

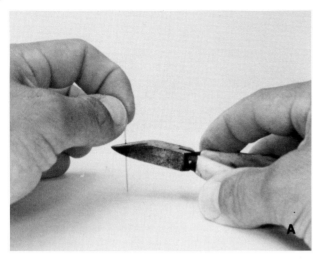

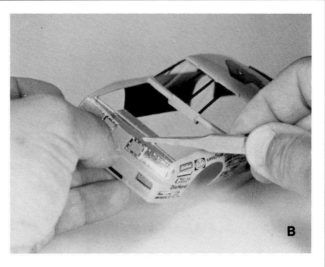

Step 5. Hood and trunk pins. Most racer kits' hoods and trunks lock with the cotter pin assembly used on '60s muscle cars. You can enhance the detail with photoetched hood and trunk pins from S & S Specialties, part No. PHP-14. But you must supply the hold-down stud that holds the cotter pin. Fine sewing needles worked well for me. Monogram's hole for the stud is too large. Fill the depressions on both the hood and trunk lids, then drill a hole the diameter of your needle. For an AMT kit, sand off the molded-in studs and drill holes there.

Next, cut your needle with diagonal cutters. Wear eye protection when you do so: Brittle needles could fly in any direction. Make sure you cut safely (**A**).

Now super glue the needle piece from the underside of the body. Use the holes drilled in the hood to guide where to glue the studs to the frame (**B**). Soak the sheet in lacquer thinner to separate the photoetched parts from the backing sheet. Both Floquil Dio-Sol and auto lacquer thinners work — as will nail polish remover, but it takes longer. When the photoetched parts come off the backing sheet, fish them out with tweezers. Careful with the cotter pins — they're extra-fragile.

After the needles set, super glue the chrome washer over the hole. (White glue will work too.) Thread the cotter pins into the studs with tweezers. A droplet of Future floor wax placed on the pin will secure it.

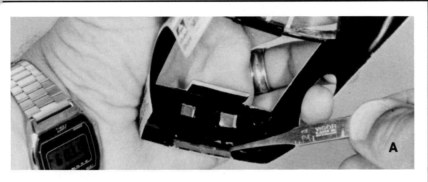

Step 6. Adding screening to grilles. Cottage industries market photoetched scale grilles and duct covers in profusion. I base my picks for car models on a grille's possibilities, regardless of its intended use. For example, some Tripart screens and covers for 1/48 scale aircraft (No. B-1) enhance a 1/24 scale Oldsmobile as much as a 1/48 scale F-4 Phantom. Tripart and other manufacturers offer entire sheets of fine screening for covering large or odd-shaped openings.

Highlight a photoetched screen's effect by drilling and filing to remove the kit's molded screen. Next cut sheet screening to fit the opening, or fit a pre-shaped piece in place. Decide how to mount the screening: on the surface of the shell; from the inside of the shell; or sandwiched between two kit pieces.

On the Kodak Olds nose, the headlamp screen covers grillwork sandwiched between the body shell and the chromed cover. For added realism, I drilled out the body shell, the headlamp covers, and the oil-cooler duct on the lower right-front part of the nose. I sanded behind the molded-in screen to remove it, which also thinned the part to accommodate the photoetched grillwork. Last, I glued the front air dam's lowest intake from the inside of the body shell (**A**). In each case, use glue sparingly to hold the screens in place. Sand, file, and cut each part; test fit until the fit is good.

Step 7. Adding labels for effect. Labels on racer models don't all have to be readable: Their mere presence adds realism. For instance, you can use many items from Micro Scale's No. 87-48, Diesel Locomotive Data sheet: Just don't use obvious no-no's like "NO STEP" or "Diesel Fuel Only." Good locations are dashboards and equipment such as oil coolers, fire extinguishers, and filters. Use your imagination.

Labels may seem trivial, but their overall impact can be great (**A**). The next section will demonstrate that.

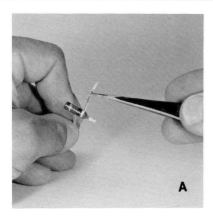 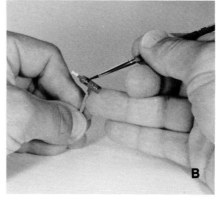 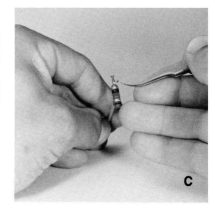

Step 8. Fire extinguisher details. Almost every racer carries a fire extinguisher and other cylinders or rectangles: oil filters, air cleaners, NOS bottles, or batteries. The variety of colors that you add will create a detailed effect.

First take one ordinary extinguisher and remove all the seam lines and other mold marks by carefully filing and sanding the part. Don't flatten any section with excessive sanding or filing.

Next, prime the part with flat-white primer, either spray or brush. When the primer is dry, check the part for flaws under a good light. Make necessary corrections and reprime. Then pick the appropriate color and apply a smooth coat.

When the paint is dry, decorate the item with a few of the decals discussed above (**A**). The real thing should be your guide.

Once the decals dry, wrap the piece with decorative striping tape for strapping (**B**). Use chrome, aluminum, or black — or Bare-Metal Foil that you have cut into thin strips.

Judicious detail painting will help the effect. For example, I painted the aluminum extinguisher head on the Kodak car.

Add a small gauge from a 1/72 scale aircraft decal sheet. Attach it — backing paper and all — with a small drop of white glue (**C**). After the dial is dry, apply a dot of Future floor wax or clear gloss to the dial's face.

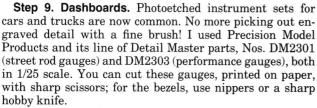

Step 9. Dashboards. Photoetched instrument sets for cars and trucks are now common. No more picking out engraved detail with a fine brush! I used Precision Model Products and its line of Detail Master parts, Nos. DM2301 (street rod gauges) and DM2303 (performance gauges), both in 1/25 scale. You can cut these gauges, printed on paper, with sharp scissors; for the bezels, use nippers or a sharp hobby knife.

Before starting, however, use a file or a hobby knife to remove the bezels molded into your dashboard. Then cut out an instrument face and glue it on the dash with a spot of white glue (**A**). Press all the glue from under the instrument so it lies flat, and allow it to dry.

To remove the bezel surround, first lay the tree on a piece of wide masking tape, sticky side up: The parts won't travel far when you (carefully!) remove them (**B**), and you can pick them up with a needle-nose tweezer.

I used 5-minute epoxy to glue the bezel to the instrument panel. First dab the epoxy on a scrap of plastic. Use the tweezers to brush the bezel through the epoxy; collect only a thin layer as you go (**C**). Then place the bezel on the dashboard and let it dry.

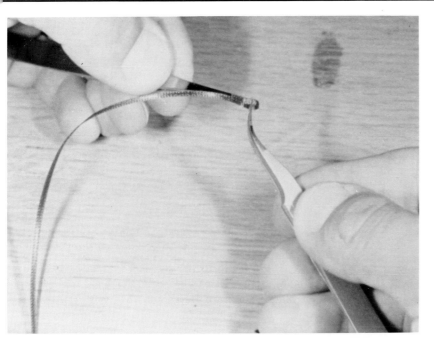

Step 10. Seat belt harness. Model aircraft cockpits are good sources for detailing seats. A caveat: Racer harnesses are bolted to the frame or chassis—not to the seat, as airplane harnesses are for ejectability. (Some racer harnesses may wrap through or drape over the seat.)

Keep scale differences in mind when you borrow aircraft parts. A 1/72 scale aircraft harness will look like masking tape on a 1/25 scale auto seat.

In the typical auto-model scales of 1/24 or 1/25, you need genuine fabric with a tight weave for the proper look. As with other detailing, the techniques build one upon the other.

I used Detail Master's buckle set, No. 2260, with decorative trim ribbon from S & S Specialities (SB-9 Seat Belting) as the belt material; you can also buy ribbon by the foot at a fabric store.

One brand of harness set will differ slightly from another, so follow the instructions supplied. Work on a well-lit table and use good tweezers. Hold the part with one pair of tweezers and thread the ribbon with another (**A**). To prevent unraveling, moisten the ribbon slightly when threading it.

Build the harness in sections, add it to the painted and finished seat, and then add the assembly to the chassis. Remember that a complete harness actually contains four to six strips of ribbon with one or two photoetched parts on each one. And make the tail end of the ribbon strip extra long for post-installation trimming. You can also take liberties with your model harness. It doesn't have to work — it only needs to look as if it does.

Ribbon seat belts don't droop like real ones. Try anchoring the belt with tiny spots of glue to simulate gravity's pull. (Too much glue will stain your fabric.)

Glue the entire assembly in place once you have tacked the harness strips to the seat. After the glue dries, trim away excess ribbon and glue the ends to anchor points on the chassis.

And there you have it. See if these 10 hints don't make your racers more competitive. **FSM**

SOURCES

- Decal stripping: Bare-Metal Foil & Hobby Co., P.O. Box 82, Farmington, MI 48024
- Photoetched instruments, seatbelt harness: Detail Master, P.O. Box 1465, Sterling, VA 22170
- Tripart photoetched grilles: available from Marco Polo Import, 532 S. Coralridge Place, Industry, CA 91746
- Diesel locomotive data sheet: Microscale Industries, 1555 Placentia Ave., Newport Beach, CA 92663
- Tire stencils: Replicas and Miniatures Co. of Maryland, 7479-D Furnace Branch Road, Glen Burnie, MD 21061
- Photoetched hood and trunk pins, seat belt trim: S & S Specialities, P.O. Box 222, Bedford, TX 76095

Extra details and added equipment really bring this 1/35 scale Sherman to life.

Basics of detailing armor models

Techniques to improve kit-built vehicles

BY HAL SANFORD

THE FEATURE that always impresses me most about superdetailed models is the abundance of tiny pieces of plastic, wire and lead foil, and gnat-sized bolts. The first time I saw one of these I remember thinking the builders must be magicians or from a different planet. As I talked with many of these magicians, I realized their detailing techniques were fairly simple — and well within the abilities of average, steady-handed builders.

If you've never tried your hand at detailing, don't be concerned about your level of ability. I'm not talking about elaborate scratchbuilding, blueprint drawing, or resin casting. Instead, we'll use several basic techniques that can be applied to substantially enhance any model's appearance.

Materials. Most detailing materials are common and inexpensive: modeling knives (No. 11 and 16 blades), round jeweler's files, a pin vise and drill bits, straightedge, brass wire, round-wound guitar strings, sheet plastic, plastic mesh screen, facial tissue, lead fo sandpaper, Grandt Line bolts, cla glue, and straight pins.

You'll also need reference materia because it is the key to creating reali tic effects. If you can see the detail a its location, you can model it more e fectively. Books from Squadron/Sign Publications, Osprey's Vanguard s ries, Tanks Illustrated, and others a available. Two other items are usef but expensive: a motor tool and th Waldron Punch and Die set.

Hull detail. Let's begin by detailir the hull underside. You won't need th holes provided for the motor, so fi them with putty or sheet plastic. Occ sionally, you can find pictures of tar undersides as I did for the Panther. U ing the picture as a guide, I traced a cess panels onto sheet plastic with circle template (available at art stores cut them out roughly with a modelir knife, and sanded the edges. I the drilled small holes with a pin vise ar added bolt heads. Another nice touch to close off the hull sponsons with she plastic. None of this was tricky, but produced a convincing replica, Fig.

Fig. 2. These materials are used to make new hatches. Grandt line bolts provide bolt head detail. The handle is lead foil.

Fig. 3. A completed dust cover on an Israeli M48. Hal uses facial tissue soaked with white glue to simulate the fabric.

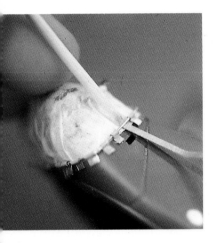

Fig. 4. The M48 dust cover under construction. Lead foil strips are bent around a brass wire to make the retaining fittings.

Fig. 1. A Panther underside with motorization holes filled and access panels added.

not a plastic toy with holes in the bottom.

Hulls can be given a realistic pitted texture by tapping them with a small, circular grinding bit (Dremel Engraving Cutter No. 106 or 107) used at low speed. This pitted texture simulates the heavy look of rolled-steel armor. Accentuate the texture by applying a dark wash over the base coat, then highlighting with a lighter shade during dry-brushing. Don't forget to consult that reference material. The surface of a Tiger tank is a lot rougher than the smooth aluminum surface found on an M113!

The tracing method also can be used to create new hatches. Cut the basic hatch from sheet styrene using the kit part as a guide, then add handles and bolts. Liquid glue is brushed on the hatch, then each bolt head (Grandt Line Products) is picked up with a glue-dampened brush and positioned on the hatch, Fig. 2.

One final point on hull details: You can often use the box art as reference. I used Tamiya's excellent cover painting of the Challenger as a guide while adding fender detail and wipers to the vision blocks.

Canvas dust covers. A dust cover is an eye-catching addition to an armor model. I've included a fairly simple dust cover on an Israeli M48, Fig. 3, and an intricate one on an M41 Walker Bulldog.

The first step is to secure the mantlet to the hull; don't add the barrel yet. Gently test fit facial tissue over the mantlet, making it slightly larger than the finished cover. Using a sharp knife, cut out holes for the barrel and any other large protrusions on the mantlet. Any texture that will show through the cover should be added now. I glued down bits of thick thread with super glue to produce ridges on top of the M41 cover. Some covers may be shaped and enhanced by placing clay under the tissue.

Mix a 50-50 solution of white glue and water and apply it to the cover with a brush. Drying can be accelerated with a hair dryer. You want the cover to look realistic, so the folds should be present but subtle. When dry, the tissue will have a parchment-

like texture. With the dry tissue in place, trace the outline of the cover, then cut off the excess. Be careful not to cut too deep and score the plastic.

The next step is to model the cover retaining device using brass wire and lead foil. Bend the wire around the mantlet and secure it either by tension or with a small amount of glue. Now comes the tedious part; the main requirements are steady hands and patience. Cut several strips of foil close to the width of the fittings; exact size isn't important. Gently slide them under the brass wire, bend them around with a toothpick, Fig. 4, and cut off the section. Make enough strips to go around the mantlet, then secure each with a drop of super glue. The sections can be trimmed to the precise size after they've been glued down.

Restraining bolts can be depicted with either Grandt Line products or disks made with the Waldron Punch and Die Set. Use a brush dampened with liquid plastic cement to help position the bolts and secure each with another drop of super glue. Finally, the fixtures for the rectangular opening

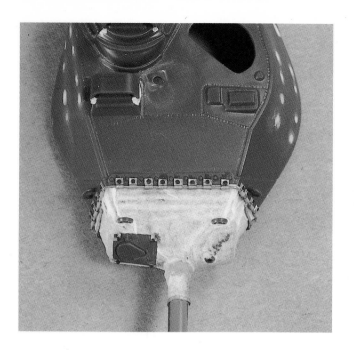

Fig. 6. Plastic mosquito netting provided the screens used ove the intakes and grilles on this 1/35 scale Tiger tank.

Fig. 5. The completed M48 dust cover prior to painting. Clay i added at the base of the barrel to build it up slightly.

were made by cutting small, L-shaped pieces of lead foil and topping each with a Grandt Line bolt.

After the mantlet was completed, I added the barrel and applied a small amount of clay to the base of the barrel to build up the cover's appearance. This was also covered with the white glue and water solution, Fig. 5.

Engine decks. Protective screens over the engine grilles are easy but attractive additions. Several materials may be used: Clover House screen plastic, brass screen, or mosquito netting. Netting is the easiest to cut but sometimes brass or plastic will provide the proper pattern. Place a rough-cut piece over the grille, mark the final shape, and place the screen on a hard surface to cut it. I used mosquito netting screens on the Tiger II, Fig. 6; the finished screens were glued in place with liquid cement.

While close to the engine, let's look at gas cap locks and restraining chains. Angled rods secured to the hull with

chain are sometimes used to lock exterior filler caps. Modeling these simply requires a small piece of bent plastic or wire and a fine-gauge chain (available in model train shops), Fig. 7. If the rod and chain are molded to the rear deck, gently scrape them off with a knife: A No. 16 blade has the best shape for removing surface detail.

Handles. The problem of making several uniform handles, such as engine grille grabs, can be solved by using wire and needle-nose pliers. After marking the length of the handle, hold the wire at the spot on the pliers that gives you that length and bend the ends down. The pliers' nose tapers, so you can make any size handle. Rough cut the length, then cut the precise length with large, straight-edged nail clippers. Using a pin vise and small bit, drill holes to accept the handles. Finally, fill any gaps and sand smooth, Fig. 7.

Guitar strings and fine wines. To accurately depict the spring mount at the

base of many antennas, use round wound guitar string (say that fast! You can buy single strings at most mu sic stores; ask for round-wound D or (strings. Use a needle-nose pliers to cu the string and unravel the outer wire leaving a solid wire core. Cut the oute wire to the desired length for your ar tenna base, Fig. 8.

Lead foil is one of my favorite detai ing materials. You can use thin shee plastic, but for making small hinges cylindrical shapes, and 90-degree bends foil is unsurpassed. Some hobby deal ers sell lead foil, but many wine bottle also have lead foil around their necks where you can obtain it for free (i doesn't come on screw-cap vintages).

The front of my M36 tank destroye was spruced up by adding steps mad from lead foil, Fig. 9. Affix the strip with any cyanoacrylate glue (supe glue). Cylindrical fender hinges can b made by bending strips around variou thicknesses of wire. The sighting de vice on my Sherman was fashioned b

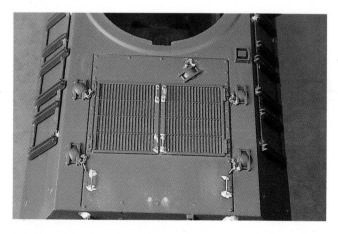

Fig. 7. The back end of this M36 has gas cap locks and the added chain. Also note the wire handles.

Fig. 8. This antenna mount was made from the outer portion of a guitar string. It definitely adds a nice touch to the model.

ending a foil strip at 90-degree angles and drilling out the sighting holes. Several Grandt Line bolts complete the sight, Fig. 10.

Wire. Brass wire can be used for fragile details such as periscope guards. It may be easier to omit them or settle for those provided in the kit, but rendering such items in scale thickness really sets a model off. The guards on my Sherman were made from brass wire, Fig. 10. I formed the sides first, glued them to the hull, and then glued the top connecting braces using super glue.

Suspension. References can also help you detail the suspension. While building a Sherman I found pictures of grooves worn into the road wheels by pressure on the track pads. I filed these grooves into the wheels and had something extra on my model, Fig. 11. I also found that the front plate of each suspension unit had four holes, so I added these with the pin vise.

How can you ensure that a tracked vehicle will sit level? Sometimes it's nearly impossible, and nothing looks stranger than a model representing tons of steel levitating over its tracks. I can hear the snickers from airplane builders out there; remember, you usually only deal with three wheels, but armor buffs deal with dozens of wheels per project. Try placing tire balancing weights inside the hull to gently push the vehicle down, or conceal the problem by putting the tank on a base and pressing the model into the terrain.

Be patient, practice, and don't let the perfectionist syndrome kill your modeling fun. If you can't get something to look right and you've exhausted your patience, move on and finish the kit. But give yourself a chance to experiment with new techniques. Above all, don't try all these techniques on your first model; pick one detail that strikes you as manageable and try that. Soon you'll be creating beautifully detailed models — just like those magicians I told you about. **FSM**

SOURCES

● Tanks Illustrated Series: Arms and Armour Press, P. O. Box 1831, Harrisburg, PA 17105
● Plastic screen: Clover House, Box 62D, Sebastopol, CA 95473
● Bolt heads: Grandt Line Products, 1040B Shary Court, Concord, CA 94518
● Vanguard series: Osprey, 27a Floral Street, London WC2E 9DP, England
● Armor in Action series: Squadron/Signal Publications, 1115 Crowley Drive, Carrollton, TX 75011
● Lead foil: Verlinden, Letterman & Stok, Lone Star Industrial Park, 811 Lone Star Drive, O'Fallon, MO 63366
● Punch and die set: Waldron Model Products, P. O. Box 431, Merlin, OR 97532

Fig. 9. Lead foil from a wine bottle (foreground) provided the steps on this M36.

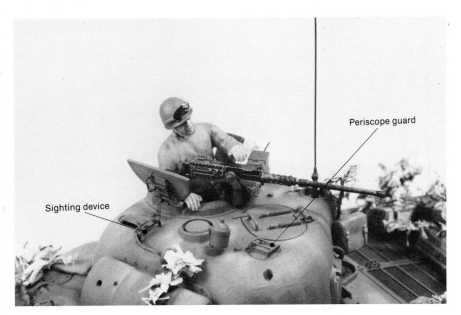

Fig. 10. This Sherman is enhanced by added details such as a wire periscope guard.

Fig. 11. References showed these wheel grooves and small holes added to a Sherman.

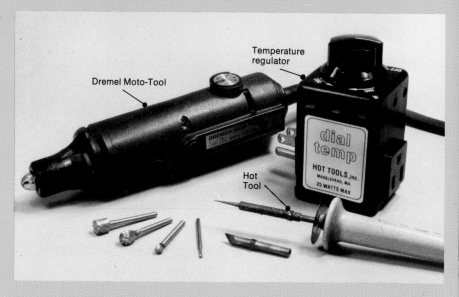

Our author calls the scene at right a German tanker's version of an Excedrin headache. The tools used to create this battle damage are shown in Fig. 1, above. The temperature regulator is an optional attachment for the Hot Tool.

Battle damage for armored vehicles

Simple techniques for modeling combat wear and tear

BY HAL SANFORD

ARMOR EXPOSED to the realities of combat seldom remained free from battle damage, and that damage is worth modeling. Don't use battle damage to hide construction or painting flaws though; more often than not it will accentuate, not conceal, such flaws. The damage I'll describe is confined to conventional steel armor; I don't know what damage would look like on new composite armor.

Damage to armor plate. Apart from entering through an open hatch, an antitank round can either punch or melt its way into a vehicle. Armor-piercing (AP) shot relies on high velocity to drive its core through the armor plate. Low-velocity High-Explosive Anti-Tank rounds (HEAT) explode on the armor surface and concentrate a focused stream of hot gases and liquid metal through the armor. Depending on the shot's velocity and the angle at which it strikes the surface, the armor will either be penetrated or gouged.

I use a Hot Tool woodburning tool (about $20.00) with a No. 8-X needle

tip to melt my way through plastic armor, Fig. 1. The needle tip is an extra part (an angled tip is standard), but it's inexpensive.

The Hot Tool is as light as a pen, so make a stand or have another means of ensuring that it doesn't roll around on your workbench. The tool takes sev-

eral minutes to cool down, so be caref' when handling it, but use your finge instead of pliers to change tips as tl heating element is delicate.

The Hot Tool can be plugged into wall outlet or a temperature regulat can be added, Fig. 1. Precise heat co trol isn't essential for modeling pen-

Fig. 2. This Su-122's fender was heated and bent to give it a used look.

ating or gouging shots, but it will be useful for small arms damage.

I suggest practicing on an old or inexpensive model. That way, you can develop your modeling skills without risking destroying a good model.

Fenders. Most fenders were made from sheet metal, so they really got banged up. New fenders can be vacuum formed over the kit parts, or you can work with the kit parts. For bends and dents, slowly heat the fender over a candle, then use a pencil eraser to bend the softened plastic, Fig. 2. The heat will cause the fenders to lose their sharp edges, so touch-up scraping with a modeling knife will be necessary.

After shaping the fenders, you can add small arms or shrapnel holes by thinning the back of the fender with sandpaper or a motor tool with high-speed cutter, Fig. 3. Thin the plastic until light shows through it, then poke through the paper-thin plastic with a screwdriver or knife to create holes.

Small arms fire. Machine gun fire didn't penetrate armor, but it did leave an impression. Re-creating this effectively requires the heat regulator I mentioned earlier. Use low power with

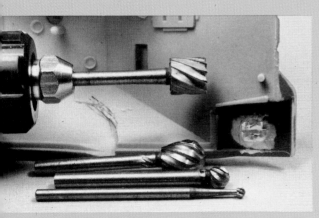

Fig. 3. A motor tool was used to thin this fender from the inside. Holes were then punched through it.

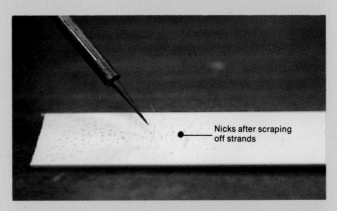

Nicks after scraping off strands

Fig. 4. The slight scrape from small arms fire is re-created with the Hot Tool used on a low temperature setting. The strings of plastic are easily scraped away.

Fig. 5. Hal pushes a needle-tipped Hot Tool straight in perpendicular to the surface to make a penetrating shot hole.

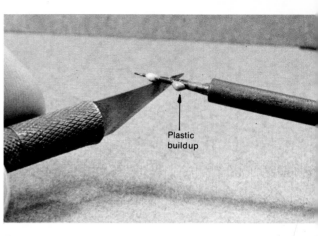

Fig. 6. Remove built-up plastic from the needle between each use to prevent it from fouling your hole.

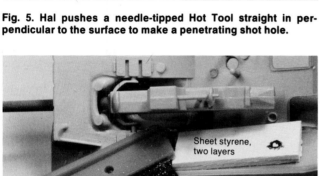

Fig. 7. The inside of the plate to be damaged is built up with sheet styrene so it will be thick enough to gouge.

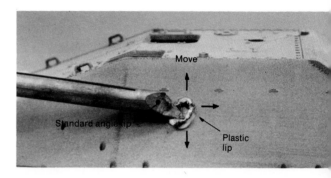

Fig. 8. The standard tip is used to create a shot gouge in the armor. Don't make the gouge too deep.

either tip; again, practice to find the correct temperature. Gently poke the plastic randomly while holding the tool at a 45-degree angle, Fig. 4. Small strands of melted plastic will be left behind but they can be scraped off with your fingernail.

You can also use the heat controller for delicate work such as accentuating

Fig. 9. Thinned putty is painted into the rough gouge to smooth out the interior and better simulate gouged metal.

weld marks. It allows you to precisely control the heat of the tip so you don't melt through the plastic or produce melted plastic lip buildup.

An alternative way to produce these shallow gouges and small scrapes is to gently bounce a motor tool high-speed cutter over the surface. The high-speed cutter bit can also be used to add pitted

texture on heavy cast-armor surfaces.

Penetrating shot. To simulate a shot that has penetrated the armor I gently push the Hot Tool needle tip in perpendicular to the surface. Through experimentation, you may find that different insertion speeds work better for you. This is where practice on sheet plastic or an old model is valuable. My test hole, Fig. 5, didn't produce a raised lip of melted plastic around the hole but you'll often get one. Just cut it off with an X-acto knife; I prefer a No. 1 blade because the blade angle allows you to work without cutting into the surrounding area. The area around the hole should be nearly flush on most penetrating shots.

Be sure the tip is free of melted plastic before making your hole. Keeping the tip clean will reduce plastic buildup around the hole — and minimize the smell of melted plastic. Use the back of an X-acto blade to gently scrape melted plastic off the tip when the tool is still warm, Fig. 6. It's easier to remove the plastic when it's hot and soft, and you're less likely to damage the tip.

Most photos indicate a darkened, irregularly shaped area extending several inches from the entry hole.

Gouges. Unfortunately for Allied tankers, German heavy tanks had frontal armor more than seven inches thick. As a result, head-on shots did lit-

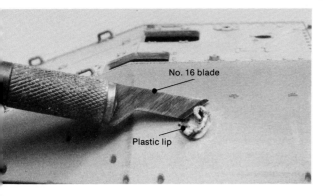

Fig. 10. Trim most of the raised lip; you want just a small ridge.

Fig. 11. This crack was made by scoring the plastic on the inside, then bending it until it cracked.

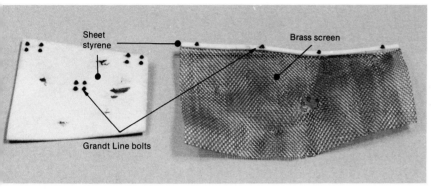

Fig. 12. Here are examples of both plate and mesh side skirts.

...e more than announce the Allied ...nk's presence to the German crew.

If you are modeling a German heavy ...nk, like the Tiger II, a nice touch is to ...ld a gouge or two to the frontal armor. ...heck your references to verify that a ...eep gouge is realistic. For example, ...e Hetzer had only 20 mm of side ar- ...or, so a shot like the one on my prac- ...ce tank would probably be too deep. ...evertheless, the techniques are iden- ...cal to those used on the Tiger II.

The first step is to increase the thick- ...ess of the kit's plastic so the gouge can ...e deep enough without going through. ...egin by adding thick sheet plastic be- ...ind the plate to be worked on, Fig. 7. I ...se Zap super glue to attach sheet, be- ...use it sets quickly.

Use the standard angled tip on the ...ot Tool for gouging. Gently press the ...p, with the point down, into the hull ...de, Fig. 8. Move the tool around ...ightly, then remove it.

You'll probably get a pronounced lip ...f melted plastic around the hole, and a ...ugh interior to the gouge. Before ...utting the Hot Tool away, try to ...nooth out the gouge interior. Apply ...inned-down putty with a brush to ...nooth out the inside of the gouge, Fig.

9. Then use your No. 16 blade to cut off most of the lip, Fig. 10.

Cracked armor. Sometimes the force of an armor-piercing round could crack a plate inward, or an interior explosion would blow a plate out. I worked from a photograph of a Hetzer knocked out by a bazooka during the Battle of the Bulge when I made the cracked plate shown in Fig. 11. I penciled the crack pattern on the inside of the model and scored the plastic with a modeling knife. Then I placed my thumb and forefinger on either side of the cut and bent the area back and forth slowly un- til a crack appeared along the scribed line.

Skirt armor. Many German vehicles carried 5 mm armor plates hung from rails to protect the turret and hull from shaped-charge grenades and bazooka rockets. Turrets were usually protected by 8 mm of armor. The rigors of battle often caused these skirts to come off or be peppered with holes from heavy ma- chine guns and armor-piercing rounds.

I replace kit-supplied parts with .020" sheet styrene and Grandt Line bolts, Fig. 12. Sand the edges of the new skirt to scale thickness. Holes through the skirt can be made with a hobby knife,

Hot Tool, compass point, or small drill. The plate can be bent slightly to give it a battlefield feel. Don't overdo bending, though, as the plate would be torn off before it was bent drastically.

As the war drew to a close, raw mate- rial shortages forced the Germans to replace plate armor with heavy wire mesh. To simulate this I use brass screen with a styrene strip and Grandt Line bolts, Fig. 12. Remember to use photo references: The only vehicle I know that used wire mesh was the Panzer IV J.

Adding battle damage to a model will often provide that "something ex- tra" to make it an attention getter. The techniques are simple. Practice is the secret to using them effectively. **FSM**

SOURCES

● Scale bolt heads: Grandt Line Prod- ucts, 1040B Shary Court, Concord, CA 94518
● Hot Tool and regulator: Hot Tool Inc., 7 Hawkes Street, P.O. Box 615, Mar- blehead, MA 01945

REFERENCES

Reference is important for modeling battle damage correctly; I've listed sev- eral books that are useful.

● Auerbach, William, *Last of the Pan- zers*, Arms and Armour Press, Poole, Dorset, England, 1984
● Culver, Bruce, *Panther in Action*, Squadron/Signal Publications, Carroll- ton, Texas, 1975
● Lefevre, Eric, *Panzers in Normandy: Then and Now*, After the Battle, 1983
● Paine, Sheperd, *Modeling Tanks and Military Vehicles*, Kalmbach Books, Milwaukee, Wisconsin, 1982
● Quarrie, Bruce, *Panzers in the Bal- kans and Italy*, Aztex Corporation, 1981

Fig. 1. Tanks in service carry everything from soup to nuts.

BASIC TECHNIQUES ✦ ADVANCED RESULTS

Modeling stowed equipment on military vehicles

The art of clutter

BY HAL SANFORD

ONE OF THE EASIEST ways to realistically enhance armor models is to add plenty of externally stowed gear, Fig. 1. Since tankers live and fight in their vehicles, it's only natural that the engine decks, fenders, and turrets are stacked with tools, helmets, gasoline cans, spare road wheels, tarps, extra tread links, captured weapons, ammunition cans, boxes, buckets, and the odd case or two of liberated wine.

Tarps and bedrolls. Let's start by packing our tanker's travel trunk with two basic items: tarps and bedrolls, Fig. 2. Everybody seems to know that facial tissue soaked in white glue is an effective way to model tarps and bedrolls. However, I've seen lots of models that appear to be carrying a load of cardboard. The key is to crumple the tissue before you roll it. Add lots of creases and folds. Next, roll it and cut the ends neatly with a scissors. Poke it with the end of a paintbrush handle and crumple it again. Then tie the ends with sewing thread, dab it with a mixture of white glue and water (50-60 percent glue), and use a hair dryer to speed drying. Before the tarp is completely dry, test fit it on the vehicle. Again, use a toothpick or brush handle to crease or depress the tarp.

Another way to bind the tarp ends is to make straps from thin strips of lead foil, available at hardware or hobby stores. Two free sources of this foil are toothpaste tubes and wine bottle seals. Cut the foil into narrow strips, using an X-acto knife and a straightedge. Gently smooth the edges with fine sandpaper. Then, take a round jeweler's file and roll it across the strip to give the strap a canvas-like texture. An attractive finishing touch is to add a buckle from the Model Technologies or Waldron lines of photoetched parts.

Painting. The two main ways of painting tarps are gentle blending and dry-brushing. Gentle blending is a technique used by many figure painters that requires careful color selection and subtle brush strokes to accen-

Fig. 2. Use lead foil for packing straps.

Fig. 3. Gauze soaked in a white glue/water mixture makes good camouflage netting. The gauze looks better if you rough it up.

Steel-covered cable ends

Fig. 4. Lead foil can be used for cable ends, too.

Use wire for drawstrings

Tools

Fig. 5. Detailing the details — drawstrings and tools make a duffel bag look real. Let the bags sag in the middle.

highlights and shadows. Dry-brushing is effective and easier — I recommend it for beginners.

Apply a base coat, and flow a dark wash over that. When it dries, gently scrub the tarp with a brush that is dipped in a lighter shade of the base color and wiped almost dry. This will provide highlights.

Preparing and painting kit equipment. If you are new to modeling, here are a few tips for working with the equipment provided in your kit. Plastic pieces usually need to be carefully cleaned up before painting. Use an X-acto knife to gently scrape away the molding seams; use fine sandpaper (400 or 600 grit) to get into places the knife can't. A small piece of sandpaper can fit into grooves and clean up hard-to-reach areas. Use fine steel wool to make sure there are no visible seams.

Most weapons can be finished flat black, then dry-brushed with light gray or silver. Be subtle — you just want to highlight the raised portions.

On items that are not black (boxes, jerrycans, panzerfausts, grenade cases, etc.), apply a dark brown wash.

Small parts are best removed from the sprue for cleaning, but you can glue them to pins or sprue for painting. I use a cyanoacrylate adhesive (super glue) like Zap/CA. The parts snap off easily when painting is complete.

Camouflage nets. Camouflage nets lend authenticity to a fighting vehicle, Fig. 3. Flexible gauze works fine, and can be found at your local drugstore. For about $2.50 you'll have enough net to cover several armored divisions.

Like the tissue, roll it up, crease it, let the cat play with it — generally rough it up. Then cut the gauze to the desired size, bind it with string or lead foil straps, soak it in the glue mixture, dry it a bit, and test fit it on the vehicle. I usually test fit tarps and nets after the vehicle is finished, but I make sure the accessories are pretty dry so I don't leave puddles of white glue.

The advantage of tissue and gauze

over plastic is that they can be contoured like the real items. For an extra touch of realism, try draping the netting over the edge of a vehicle or over boxes so it looks like fabric.

Cables. No self-respecting tanker ventures out into the muck without tow cables. Kit cables are usually not convincing. You can best capture the heavy, metal appearance of worn cables by using shipbuilding rope. Paint it a steel color, give it a black wash, and highlight it by dry-brushing with light gray or silver. Easy does it — you want a weathered tow cable, not a chrome bumper!

The ends of the cables can be finished in several ways. One way is to cut off the plastic ends from the kit cable and glue the rope to them. A second is to loop the rope and clasp it with a strip of lead foil. My favorite method is to loop the rope, fasten it with lead foil, and add a small lead foil strip (gently creased down the middle) to the inside of the loop. This looks like the cables

Weathered chains

Fig. 6. Weather chains with Hobby Black.

Fig. 7. Herbs add spice to camouflage.

found on many World War Two German tanks, Fig. 4.

Other sources of cable are light gauge picture-hanging wire or tightly wound string. Applying wax to the string helps subdue unrealistic fuzz, but it also makes painting harder.

In the bag. Fashion sandbags and duffel bags with epoxy putty. Roll the putty into a strand, cut off small sections, and use your fingers to mold them into sandbags. Create a canvas-like texture by pressing fine-textured screen into the putty. Use the back of a hobby knife to make seams.

Form duffel bags and drape them over fenders. Make a small hole in one end with a pencil, and use wire to make drawstrings. Put tools or handles in the opening, Fig. 5.

Chains. Chains are another way to enhance your models, Fig. 6. Hook preweathered Clover House chain on a lift ring or pile it on a fender. To blacken shiny chain, dip it in Hobby Black. It darkens metals (except aluminum) without obscuring detail. The product is indispensable for finely detailed metal accessories.

More equipment. Tools add realism.

Stain shovels and picks with dabs of putty or Celluclay. Scrape off molded retaining straps and replace them with lead foil. Toss on extra tools such as wire cutters and tripods.

Model railroad shops are a good place to find scale tools. The Testor/Italeri Field Tool Shop kit is an inexpensive source of such equipment.

Extra track links look great. I've seen photographs of several types of tracks on one tank. (Tank crews use all manner of auxiliary armor to increase survivability.) Verlinden ration boxes look good, too; rough them up slightly with a razor saw.

Extra ammunition boxes are also a nice addition. They're available in the Tamiya German and American Infantry Weapons sets. Try adding writing to these and other boxes by using a fine brush to scrawl illegible but orderly looking marks. Decals provide the same effect. For example, the Microscale F-4 Phantom data sheet (No. 72-0164) has lots of illegible but effective writing.

Tree-branch camouflage. Foliage is another way to dress up armor, Fig. 7. I took branch-like roots from one of my black-thumbed horticultural failures (a deceased ficus), dabbed them in white glue, and rolled them in crumbled piles of green herbs. The leaves retained a soft green color.

Let me leave you with this thought. At times I've stopped modeling because I couldn't master sophisticated techniques. But don't despair. You don't have to be an expert — wonderful results can be achieved with basic techniques. Visit a hobby shop soon, treat yourself, and remember they are called "hobby shops" for a reason. **FSM**

SOURCES

• Celluclay: Activa Products, Marshall TX 75670
• Brass weapons: Cal-Scale, P.O. Box 322, Montoursville, PA 11754
• Pre-weathered chain: Clover House Box 62D, Sebastopol, CA 95473
• Cast-metal detail parts: Detail Associates, P.O. Box 5357, San Luis Obispo, CA 93403
• Brass screen: LMG Enterprises, 1627 S. 20th St., Sheboygan, WI 53081
• Photoetched detail parts: Model Technologies, 2761 Saturn, Brea, CA 92621
• Boxes: VLS Products, Lone Star Industrial Park, 811 Lone Star Drive, O'Fallon, MO 63366
• Photoetched detail parts: Waldron Model Products, P.O. Box 431, Merlin, OR 97532

Bob's 1/48 scale Monogram P-39F Airacobra. Note how light reflects off the acetate instrument faces. Bob has the "car door" windows cranked halfway down. Also visible is the throttle quadrant and the ring sight above the instrument panel.

Detailing aircraft cockpits

The main ingredients are tiny pieces and a bit of time

BY BOB STEINBRUNN

I FLY FOR A LIVING, so detailing the cockpit of a model is of more than average interest to me. The key to adding cockpit detail is *time* — not fantastic ability, the soul of an artist, or the hands of a watchmaker, as you may have heard. Just time.

It's all too easy to look at a photo of a real cockpit and be overwhelmed by the complexity of it all. But in detailing model aircraft cockpits, it is best to concentrate on one area at a time, finish it, and move on. I've been so frustrated by working on one thing and worrying about another that it ceased to be *fun*, and after all, fun is what modeling is all about. So instead of giving up and cementing the canopy closed, put your blinders on and work on it one step at a time.

Although I build mostly 1/48 scale World War Two aircraft, the tips in this article can be applied to jets and to other scales. I like detailing cockpits in 1/48 scale: 1/72 scale seems to me to be awfully small for this kind of treatment, but I've seen it done well. Detailing in 1/32 scale almost requires a miniature manufacturer's data plate to look right. I don't have to go overboard on the time factor cobbling up details in 1/48 scale.

If you haven't tried your hand at cockpit detailing, now is the time to select a kit worthy of your effort, and arm yourself with as many cockpit photos as you can. Before you get too far into the research, settle on a particular variant of the aircraft. It is surprising how many changes are made in instrument panels and cockpits among variants of the same type of aircraft. Some

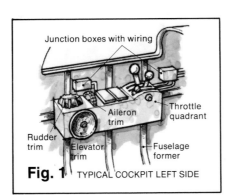

Fig. 1 TYPICAL COCKPIT LEFT SIDE

Junction boxes with wiring

Throttle quadrant

Aileron trim

Rudder trim

Elevator trim

Fuselage former

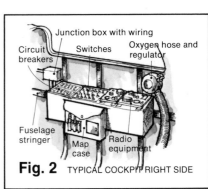

Fig. 2 TYPICAL COCKPIT RIGHT SIDE

Junction box with wiring

Circuit breakers

Switches

Oxygen hose and regulator

Fuselage stringer

Map case

Radio equipment

Detailing 55

typical examples are the differences between the F6F-3 and -5 Hellcat instrument panels, or the changes in the USAF, USMC, and Navy versions of the OV-10A Bronco. Once you have decided which version you'll build, cover your workbench with cockpit photos, plans, and drawings.

Starting out. Typically, WWII fighter cockpits had the trim wheels and the throttle control, or quadrant, on the left console or attached to the left fuselage interior structure. The radio controls, circuit breakers, and oxygen regulator with hose were usually found on the right side, Figs. 1 and 2. Of course these rules are not hard and fast, so always check reference photos for the plane you are modeling.

For easy access, cockpit detailing is best done before the fuselage halves are glued together. I start with the fuselage sides, grinding away any shallow kit detailing and mold marks with a Dremel Tool and burr. Next, I add fuselage formers and stringers with Plastruct shapes and Evergreen strip styrene. It's a good idea to periodically check the fit of the cockpit tub or seat assemblies to make sure that the added detail allows adequate clearance.

I use .010″ sheet styrene and wire or stretched sprue to simulate junction boxes and cables visible in the reference photos, and build up the consoles with sheet styrene. Throttle quadrants can be made from sheet styrene, Fig. 3. A visit to a model railroad shop can reward you with tiny photoetched brake wheels that make excellent trim wheels and landing gear cranks, Fig. 4. Small parts made for HO model railroads can be used for throttle, mixture, prop pitch, and supercharger levers, Fig. 5.

I make oxygen hoses by wrapping thin motor armature wire around thicker wire in a loose spiral, coating the resulting coil with a liquid masking agent, and painting when dry, Fig. 6.

The cockpit in this Otaki 1/48 scale Bf 109G-6 is almost entirely scratchbuilt. Note the yellow fuel line on the right side of the cockpit. Bob vacuum-formed and opened the canopy so the interior detail is easier to see.

Monogram's 1/48 scale P-47D Thunderbolt "Miss Behave" has received the cockpit detailing treatment. Note the added rearview mirror, ring and reflector gunsights, and rudder pedals.

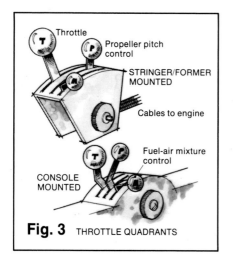

Fig. 3 THROTTLE QUADRANTS

Throttle
Propeller pitch control
STRINGER/FORMER MOUNTED
Cables to engine
Fuel-air mixture control
CONSOLE MOUNTED

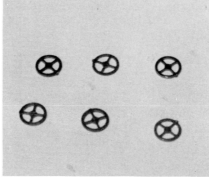
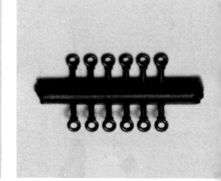

Figs. 4 and 5. (Left) Photoetched brass model railroad brake wheels make realistic trim and landing gear crank wheels. (Right) Tiny injection-molded styrene eyebolts can be used as levers on throttle quadrants and other cockpit controls. These can be found in model railroad shops.

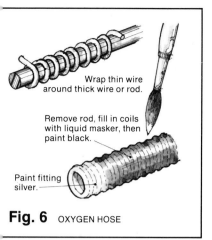

Fig. 6 OXYGEN HOSE

Wrap thin wire around thick wire or rod.

Remove rod, fill in coils with liquid masker, then paint black.

Paint fitting silver.

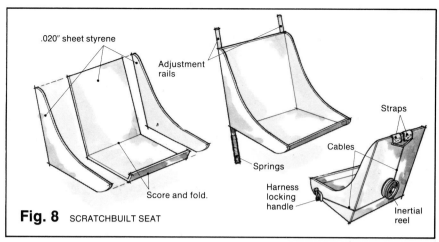

Fig. 8 SCRATCHBUILT SEAT

.020″ sheet styrene

Adjustment rails

Score and fold.

Springs

Harness locking handle

Straps

Cables

Inertial reel

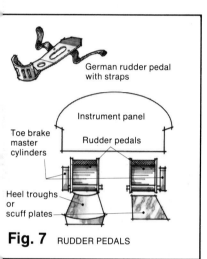

Fig. 7 RUDDER PEDALS

German rudder pedal with straps

Instrument panel

Toe brake master cylinders

Rudder pedals

Heel troughs or scuff plates

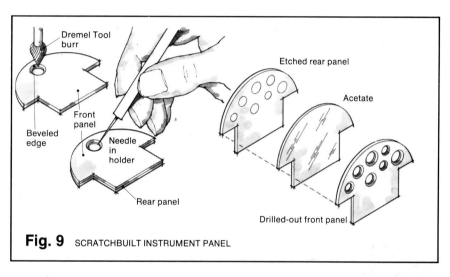

Fig. 9 SCRATCHBUILT INSTRUMENT PANEL

Dremel Tool burr

Front panel

Beveled edge

Needle in holder

Rear panel

Etched rear panel

Acetate

Drilled-out front panel

hen I bend it to shape, paint a fitting [o]n one end, and attach the other to the [re]gulator mode of a disc of sprue.

Floor and rudder pedals. Some air-[cr]aft actually had no floor at all (for ex-[am]ple, Wildcats and early Corsairs), [ju]st a seat attached to an armored [bu]lkhead with two troughs leading up [to] the rudder pedals. This arrangement can be made using Plastruct "I" beams attached to fore and aft cockpit bulkheads.

I make rudder pedals from sheet styrene cut to the appropriate shape and suspended on stretched sprue rods. Many U.S. aircraft had toe-operated main wheel brakes with master cylinders attached to the sides of the pedals.

The brakes were activated by pivoting the rudder pedals; the cylinders can be represented by using sections of sprue, Fig. 7. German rudder pedals had leather straps which can be simulated with masking tape.

Seats. Kit-supplied seats are sometimes usable, but a seat scratchbuilt from .020″ sheet styrene looks better. I build the seat in three sections which can be shaped or rounded into the particular seat desired, Fig. 8.

Some seats have height adjustment rails with springs which can be made of wire and Walther's HO railroad coil springs (part No. 945-3005). The seat belts, harness, and other straps can be made from your favorite tape, and a set of Waldron or Unique Scale buckles, although expensive, really dress up the cockpit.

U.S. aircraft featured a shoulder harness that went over the back of the seat, where the two straps joined together in a metal fitting. The fitting was attached to cable which ran down

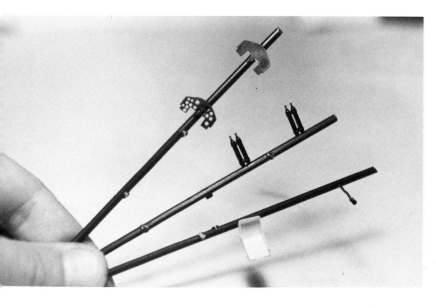

Fig. 10. Painting small parts such as instrument panels, oxygen bottles, seats, and sticks is easy when they are attached to sprues with a small drop of liquid cement.

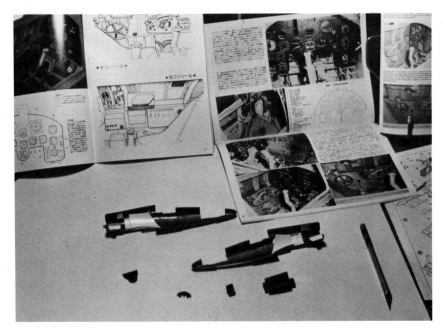

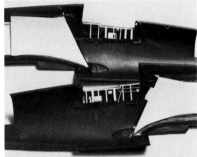

Step 2. This is the kit cockpit tub before modification. The sidewalls and floor will be cut away and replaced with more realistic structures. The sockets for the rear brace will also be trimmed away.

Step 1. Superdetailing a cockpit is not difficult if you take it one step at a time. Let's take Hasegawa's 1/48 scale Kyusho J7W1 Shinden and start by setting up reference material in a convenient location. This leaves your hands free to work on the model.

Step 3. Strip styrene and sprue simulate the cockpit side wall structure. The fuselage halves will be assembled after installation of the cockpit tub. The large white areas to the rear of the cockpit are sheet styrene that blocks off the intakes on the fuselage sides.

Step 5. Here's the kit seat (left) beside the finished scratchbuilt replacement. Note the masking tape harness and seat belts. Unique Scale brass belt buckles add realism.

Step 4. (Left) The completed cockpit tub before painting. Note the "I" beam foot troughs, and the sheet styrene radio with sprue knobs. (Right) The scratchbuilt throttle quadrant and other controls applied to the left side of the cockpit tub.

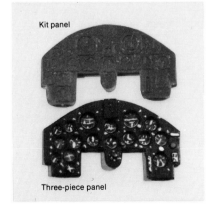

Kit panel

Three-piece panel

Step 6. Compare the kit instrument panel with its scratchbuilt counterpart. Note the added relief from the beveled edges and etched detail on the instrument faces.

Step 7. The completed cockpit tub after painting. The instrument panel, stick, and seat have been installed, and the tub is ready to be mounted in the fuselage.

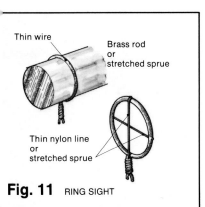

Thin wire

Brass rod
or
stretched sprue

Thin nylon line
or
stretched sprue

Fig. 11 RING SIGHT

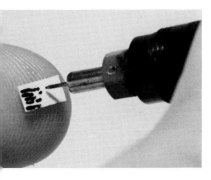

g. 12. Technical pens can draw fine lines
r miniature cockpit placards. Here is a
ny sheet styrene placard which will be at-
ched to the sidewall of a cockpit tub.

 an inertial reel on the back of the
:at. From there another cable ran to
:e harness locking handle on the left
.de of the seat pan.

Instrument panels made easy. The
istrument panel is the main ingredi-
nt of a detailed cockpit. Happily, this
 one of the few items on a model
·here a little effort yields a big divi-
end. Although the finished product

looks difficult to make, I think it's the
easiest part of the cockpit.

Start with a paper template that is
roughly the shape of the actual panel,
and fit it to the fuselage halves by trial
and error. Use the templates as a pattern to cut two blank panels from .010″
white sheet styrene, and a third from
clear acetate, Fig. 9. Drill out holes for
the instruments in one of the styrene
panels with a Dremel Tool No. 118
burr. I use this instead of a drill because the burr bevels the edges of the
holes for a more realistic appearance.

Next, paint both styrene panels flat
black. Attach these and other small
parts to sprues to make them easier to
paint, Fig. 10. Using the front panel as
a template, use a needle to scratch
through the black paint of the rear
panel. I first etch a circle around each
instrument, and then etch in the instrument markings.

Next, sandwich the clear acetate between the two styrene panels, and carefully apply white glue around the
edges. The clear acetate simulates the
glass faces of the instruments. This extra touch looks especially nice when
light reflects off the instruments. After
the panel is dry, add any additional lettering, placards, switches, and knobs.

Gunsight reflectors can also be made
from acetate. If the particular aircraft
you are modeling had a ring-and-bead
sight, wrap armature wire around a
suitable piece of brass tubing or sprue,
twist it, and remove the tube, Fig. 11.
Crosshairs can be made from small-diameter nylon thread or fine stretched
sprue. Glue the sight to the cockpit
coaming before attaching the wind
screen.

Finishing. After the subassemblies
are constructed, paint the cockpit its

main color, then paint the details. Add
stenciling and placards by painting
red, black, or white rectangles and
then adding the writing in a contrast-
ing color. A technical drafting pen,
such as a Koh-i-noor Rapidograph, is
excellent for these as well as for making stencils, Fig. 12. They have an ink
reservoir and a hollow, needle-like
point that draws a fine line. The pens
have interchangeable tips of various
widths and are available from artist's
supply stores. Inks come in many colors, but I find black, white, and red to
be most useful.

If the aircraft you are modeling has a
sliding canopy, glue two pieces of sprue
along the fuselage sides for canopy
tracks. When the cockpit is finished
and the fuselage is assembled, cover
the cockpit with a paper hood and seal
the edges with liquid masker. This
mask is easily removed after the model
is painted.

Finally, I think it's better to add too
much detail, even if you don't think it
will show once the model is assembled.
It's always more difficult to add details
after the model is finished.

There, wasn't that easy? And all it
took was time! **FSM**

SOURCES

● Plastruct: 1020 S. Wallace Place,
City of Industry, CA 91748
● Sheet styrene: Evergreen Scale Mod-
els, 12808 N. E. 125th Way, Kirkland,
WA 98034
● Wm. K. Walthers Inc., P. O. Box
18676, Milwaukee, WI 53218
● Waldron Model Products, P. O. Box
431, Merlin, OR 97532
● Unique Scale Hobbies, 1178 Boston
Road, Springfield, MA 01119

You can produce models that look as realistic as Bob's modified 1/48 scale Arii Spitfire. Bob went all out, combining aftermarket cockpit detailing sets from Fotocut, Model Technologies, and Waldron Model Products.

Installing photoetched cockpit details

A no-holds-barred remodeling of Arii's 1/48 scale Spitfire

A

B

Step 1. Pieces of the puzzle. The project began when I spied Fotocut's 1/48 scale Spitfire photoetched detail set at a recent IPMS national convention. One look and I was hooked. Parts include the seat, bulkheads, fuselage frames, pilot's door, floorboards, control column, instrument panel, and other small items (**A**). The humorous instructions tell you what the parts are, but not how to assemble everything. You'll need good references or a thousand hours flying Spitfires to figure everything out.

Adding these details is not for the beginner. Many of the metal parts require repeated test fitting. The amount of plastic you'll need to add or remove to make the details fit will vary with the particular kit that you're detailing.

Fotocut's set provides many details but not everything I wanted, so I purchased Waldron's photoetched Spitfire cockpit placards and metal parts kit (**B**). It contains one metal-foil black-and-silver placards sheet, with the throttle-quadrant face, the landing-gear (chassis) quadrant face, and various other printed faceplates for panels and controls. Also included are comprehensive instructions and two photoetched metal frames of parts. The assemblies require some thought and homemade jigs (see step 2), but they were fun to work with.

The Model Technologies kit supplies a complete photo-

Go ahead, climb in and have a look around! Bob shows you how to install photoetched detail parts such as this open cockpit door.

Y BOB STEINBRUNN

HIGH-TECH KITS offer both exceptional detail and a challenge to the builder. The price you pay is high compared with "low-tech" all-plastic kits. So how would the costs compare if you added aftermarket high-tech parts to a low-tech kit? Can you get increased detail without increasing the price? Well, yes and no.

If you consider only price, you'll lose money with this approach. The subject that I chose, the Spitfire Mk.IX in 1/48 scale, has no high-tech alternative, and my only option was to scratchbuild the detail. I spent nearly $50 on the kit and detail sets; high-tech kits of World War II fighters in this scale are generally less expensive.

You can equal the detail of a high-tech kit with aftermarket detail sets —

and more effort. Use care and patience to make the different manufacturers' parts fit.

The payoff is — fun! My project was more entertaining than merely assembling a complete high-tech kit. Engineering these kits into the Spitfire provided me with a sense of accomplishment. I'll show you how you can create a superdetailed interior to any 1/48 scale Spitfire variant.

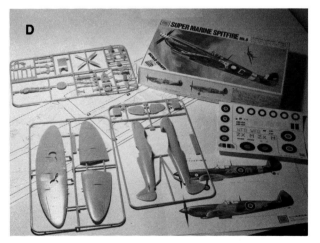

etched brass British Sutton seat harness, including seat belts, shoulder harness, buckles, and complete instructions (**C**).

Next I needed a kit for all this detail. I wanted to model a famous British Mk.IX, so I chose the Arii Spitfire Mk.VIII (**D**, ex-Otaki, also found in Ertl/AMT boxes). The particular Spitfire I chose (an early Mk.IX) required some changes, so I robbed a few parts from an old Monogram Spitfire Mk.IX (rudder, wing cannon breech fairings, and engine air intake) and a Revell Spitfire Mk.II (decal sheet with placards and stenciling; tail wheel). For markings, I used two Super Scale International de-

cal sheets (No. 72-51) for the aircraft codes (JE J).

I built the Spitfire Mk.IXc Wing Commander "Johnnie" Johnson flew when he led No. 403 and No. 416 (Canadian) Squadrons from Kenley Airfield, Surrey, England, in March 1943. His aircraft (No. EN 398) was coded "JE J," Johnson's initials, a common practice among squadron leaders.

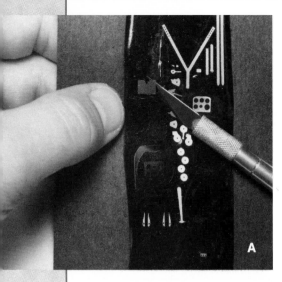

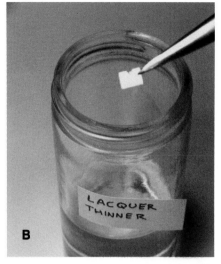

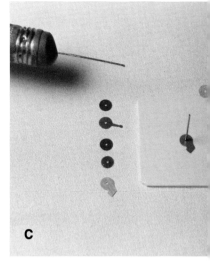

Step 2. Special tools and techniques.
Unlike most photoetched detail parts, the Fotocut parts are lacquered onto a vinyl backing sheet, not attached to sprues. The parts detach easily; use the tip of a hobby knife to carefully peel each part off the backing sheet (**A**), then use tweezers to immerse the part in lacquer thinner to dissolve the lacquer residue (**B**). Wipe the part with a clean cloth, and it's ready for assembly.

Fotocut's throttle and landing-gear quadrants require a simple homemade jig to ensure accurate alignment during assembly. I used .040″ sheet styrene and K&S .015″ piano wire for the jig (**C**). Thread the wire through the hole in each part and fasten the parts with tiny drops of super glue. Clip off excess wire from the jig. After paint-ing, the finished quadrant is ready for installation (**D**).

Hold Waldron's thin printed-metal placards with tweezers and cut each one out with sharp scissors such as Fiskars (**E**). Attach the placards with brushed-on white glue.

The metal parts in Waldron's and Model Technologies' sets are attached to frames, and separating the parts poses several problems. To avoid bending the delicate parts, place them on a metal or glass surface and cut them with a sharp blade for a clean cut (**F**). Hold the parts with tweezers so they won't go flying as you cut them free. Wear safety glasses while cutting: tiny metal bits are hazardous to your eyes. Gently sand burrs from the cut edge.

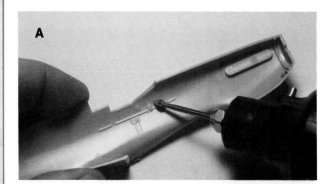

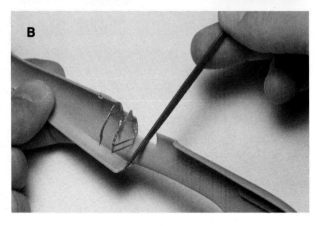

Step 3. Into the cockpit.
I used a burr bit in a motor tool to remove all molded-in cockpit details (**A**), then sanded the cockpit walls smooth. The Fotocut pilot's door consists of a dozen pieces. To use it, remove the kit door from the left fuselage half, then file the inside edges around the opening so they don't look unrealistically thick (**B**).

Install the two main fuselage frames first, since most of the other photoetched parts are positioned relative to them. To attach them with super glue, I rigged a super glue applicator by pushing a fine wire into a pencil eraser.

Assemble the pilot's door by building up the Fotocut

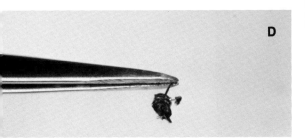

REFERENCES

- Bell, Dana, *Air Force Colors, Vol. 2, ETO & MTO 1942-1945*, Squadron/Signal Publications, Carrollton, Texas, 1980
- Brown, Cpt. Eric, *Wings of the Navy*, Jane's Publishing Company Ltd., London, 1980
- Flack, Jeremy, *Spitfire — A Living Legend*, Osprey Publishing, Ltd., London, 1985
- Gouldings, James, and Robert Jones, *Camouflage & Markings, RAF Fighter Command, Northern Europe, 1936 to 1945, Supermarine Spitfire*, Ducimus Books Ltd., London, 1970
- Green, William, *Famous Fighters of the Second World War, Volume One*, Doubleday and Co. Inc., Garden City, New York, 1965
- Johnson, Air Vice-Marshall J. E., "Supermarine Spitfire," from *In the Cockpit*, Orbis Publishing Ltd., London, 1979
- *Koku-Fan Modeling Manual, Supermarine Spitfire Mk. I-XVI*, Bunrin-Do Co. Ltd., Tokyo
- Maloney, Edward T., *Supermarine Spitfire*, Aero Publishers, Fallbrook, California, 1966
- Mason, Francis K., *Royal Air Force Fighters of World War Two*, Doubleday and Co. Inc., Garden City, New York, 1971
- Mondey, David, *British Aircraft of World War II*, The Hamlyn Publishing Group Ltd., London, 1982
- Moss, Peter, and Len Batchelor, *Supermarine Spitfire Mk.IX*, Profile Publications Ltd., Windsor, Berkshire, England, 1971
- Price, Alfred, *Spitfire — A Documentary History*, Charles Scribner's Sons, New York, 1979
- Price, Alfred, *Spitfire at War*, Ian Allan Ltd., Shepperton, Surrey, England, 1974
- Scutts, Jerry, *Spitfire in Action*, Squadron/Signal Publications, Carrollton, Texas, 1980
- Sweetman, Bill, and Rikyu Watanabe, *Spitfire*, Crown Publishers, New York, 1980

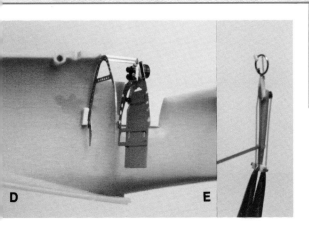

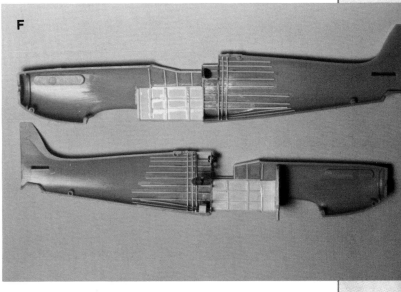

parts, then attach it with super glue (**C**). Note how the pilot's back armor and head armor are installed on small spacers. The headrest comes from a plastic propeller shaft; the white longitudinal brace supporting the two rear frames is Evergreen strip styrene formed into a T-shaped beam (**D**). Use Evergreen or Contrail .060″ rod for the voltage regulators mounted aft of the pilot's head armor.

Fotocut provides a control column, but being photo-etched, it's flat. I decided to make my own from sheet styrene, stretched sprue, and wire formed around a paintbrush handle for the round spade grip (**E**).

I made cockpit sidewalls from .010″ sheet styrene, then added frames and stringers of Evergreen strip styrene (**F**).

A

Step 4. Take your seat and buckle in. Since the Spitfire cockpit is so cramped, the seat is the most visible item within. It pays to spend time on it. The Fotocut seat is a kit in itself, and it's a beauty (**A**). Your bends in the seat pan and back have to be accurate so that the side pieces line up. Fill your seams with super glue and sand carefully when the glue is dry; the hard part will be over. You can make the seat-mounting struts, elevating mech-

anism with handle, and other details from .010″ and .020″ rod and sheet styrene.

Add the Sutton harness after the seat is painted. Bunrin-Do's *Modeling Manual, Supermarine Spitfire Mk.I-XVI* provides excellent drawings of the seat, control column, canopy mechanism, and a host of other details.

One of the keys in this project is to dry-fit sub-

SOURCES

• **Contrail rod and tubing,** available from Imported Specialties, 3655 Sullivant Ave., Columbus, OH 43228
• **Sheet, tube, and rod styrene:** Evergreen Scale models,12808 N. E. 125th Way, Kirkland, WA 98034

Photoetched detail parts:

• **Fotocut,** Erieville Road, Box 120, Erieville, NY 13061
• **Model Technologies,** 13472 Fifth St., Suite 12, Chino, CA 91710
• **Waldron Model Products,** P. O. Box 431, Merlin, OR 97532

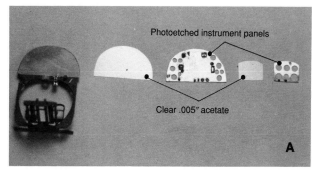

Photoetched instrument panels

Clear .005″ acetate

A

Step 5. Flying on instruments. The Fotocut kit provides almost everything you need for the instrument panels, including two different styles of the blind-flying panels. The Waldron kit provides some extra switches, levers, and instrument bezels you can add to the Fotocut panel. For that extra touch, cut thin acetate sections from a clear page protector, sized to fit beneath the instrument panels; these represent the glass gauge covers (**A**).

Paint the rear panel flat black; then, using the front panel as a template, scribe the instrument markings through the paint with a needle. (See "Sprucing up the Arii Willow," January 1990 FSM.) When all is assembled, painted, and detailed, the panel looks realistic (**B**).

The reflector gunsight frame is from Waldron's 1/48 scale photoetched seat belt and shoulder harness kit, and the reflector glass is made from thin acetate attached with white glue (**C**).

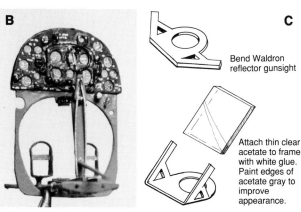

B

C

Bend Waldron reflector gunsight

Attach thin clear acetate to frame with white glue. Paint edges of acetate gray to improve appearance.

I made the rearview mirror atop the windscreen bow from two Fotocut parts, attached it with white glue, and painted the mirror face with Testor silver.

The Fotocut kit supplies the butterfly latch handle inside the sliding hood (canopy).

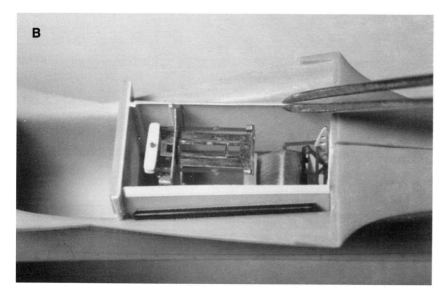

B

C

assemblies together frequently in order to uncover clearance problems while you still have access to them. I had to dry-fit the seat and floorboards into the fuselage halves about ten times until I had all clearance problems resolved. To duplicate the lower curve of the fuselage sides inside the cockpit under the floorboards, I had to add sheet styrene strips fore and aft to the cockpit side walls (**B**).

I used Model Technologies' harness set, with its buckles, adjusting holes in the belts, release handles with cables, and other details. I assembled the Sutton harness lap belts, shoulder harness, buckles, and attaching hardware, then painted them and attached them to the seat with white glue. I assembled the Fotocut pilot's signal-flare cartridge holder, then laminated, painted, and attached sheet styrene to the front of the seat pan (**C**).

Step 6. Final details. After adding most of the details to the sidewalls, I airbrushed the cockpit Humbrol British Interior Grey-Green. With a 3 x 0 technical drawing pen, I applied gray ink along the interior stringers, ribs, and frames where they met the fuselage side wall. By providing relief and shadow, the detail appears more three-dimensional. Black ink would have been too harsh.

Add the final details, paint them, and attach all the placards with white glue. Insert various sizes of styrene rod for wires, cables, rods, and tubes. You can make the silver oxygen tank and charging bottles for the guns by filing down a rocket from your spare parts box.

I vacuum formed my canopy and added a thin piece of clear plastic for the windscreen armor. That finishes the Spitfire interior, a realistic assembly of the best after-market detail sets available. **FSM**

With the fuselage apart, we see the left side of the finished cockpit, including the photoetched seat.

The right side of the cockpit. Note the Waldron printed placards and the instrument panel with its clear acetate gauge covers.

Detailing small-scale ship models

Aftermarket photoetched and injection-molded parts make for major improvements

Craig posed the finished *Shikinami* on textured plastic made by Preiser to simulate water for railroad layouts. A spotlight high and to the left is the main light and a small reflector card to the right fills in the shadows. A blue card out of the scene to the rear provides sky reflections on the "waves." Note the photoetched crew figures manning the rails.

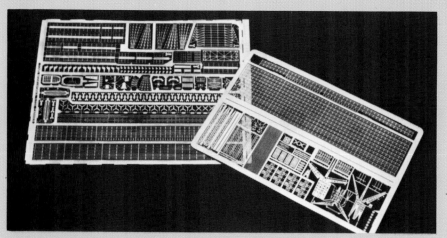

Fig. 1. Photoetched detail parts can enhance any small-scale ship model. Here are a U. S. carrier set from Tom's Modelworks (left) and a U. S. cruiser/destroyer set from Gold Medal Models, both for 1/700 scale ships.

BY CRAIG SCOGIN

MANY MODELERS find it impo sible to complete a kit witho some modification or conversion as a expression of individuality. The ava ability of commercial detail and co version parts has opened up new leve of challenge and personal choice. F 1/700 scale naval modelers photoetch metal and injection-molded produc are now available.

I had been satisfied that standa 1/700 scale kits were fairly realistic some details were slightly heavy, b the overall impression was good. Ph tographs of real ships indicate th deck railings, for example, are pract cally invisible at normal viewing di tances. Photoetched metal parts, ho ever, add a level of fine, transpare

"Bearing, mark! Range: 9½ divisions in high power. Down scope! Angle on the bow, port 90. Prepare tubes 3 and 4 for firing." *Shikinami* as she may have looked before U. S. S. *Growler* sunk her in September 1944.

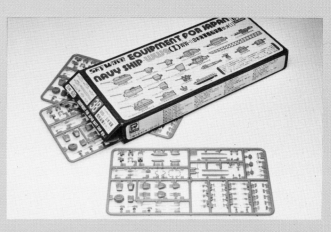

Fig. 2. Skywave produces alternate shipboard weapon sets for 1/700 waterline ship models. This is set No. 38, which Craig used to detail his Tamiya *Shikinami*.

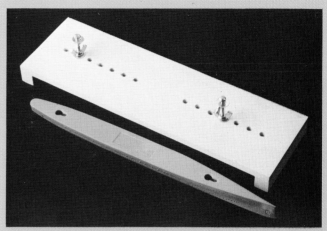

Fig. 3. Craig made this handy stand to hold his ship models as he adds detail. The wing nuts are shown on top of the stand here, but are placed below when the model is mounted on the stand. The bolts fit in the holes drilled in the bottom of the hull. When finished, Craig loosens the wing nuts and slides the model off the stand.

etail and new injection-molded parts re better detailed than the original aterline kit parts, Fig. 1.

I used photoetched stainless steel arts from Gold Medal Models (GMM) r these projects. These included the nperial Japanese Navy (IJN) Cruiser/ estroyer set (No. 700-13), Naval Ship t (boat pulleys), and Anchor/Chain t. GMM also offers a handbook de- cribing detail parts and their applica- on. New injection-molded parts came om Skywave's IJN Weapons set (No. 8), Fig. 2. Skywave also has weapons r cruisers and destroyers (No. 47) and odern naval weapons (Nos. 32 and 37).

Let's start with an apparently simple estroyer kit, the Tamiya *Shikinami* No. 053). Ordinarily a three- or four- our project, this small ship demon- rates most of my detailing techniques. The *Shikinami* is a fundamentally ound kit of a *Fubuki*-class destroyer as was equipped late in World War Two. o portholes are molded on the hull nd superstructure, so we'll have to

drill them out. Additional single 13 mm and 25 mm antiaircraft (AA) mounts will be added from the detailing parts.

Photoetched parts should be cut and bent to shape before installation. Test fit replacement injection-molded parts to determine if they need adjustment to fit properly. Because of the overall gray scheme of Japanese Navy destroyers, most assembly can be completed before painting. Details are painted on after spraying the overall color. If the deck is a different color than the hull, I assem- ble and paint superstructure compo- nents separately, then add them after painting the hull.

I plan construction to work from the inside out, beginning with hull/super- structure elements and working out- ward so components that are most likely to be damaged in handling are added last. Also important are any parts that pass through another; be- ware of trying to weave parts with glue on them.

Tools and materials. Along with the

usual modeling tools (X-acto knives and sandpaper), you'll need manicure scissors for cutting photoetched parts, dividers for measuring, and tweezers or small square-nose pliers for bending sharp corners. Rounded corners or curves are bent around a tube or cylin- der having a slightly smaller diameter than desired, to allow for the springi- ness of the metal parts.

I use Duro Quick Gel, a gel-type cyanoacrylate adhesive, for mounting photoetched parts because it doesn't run. Apply several beads to the joint, spread them out with a wood stick, and position the part with tweezers. Con- ventional plastic liquid cement is my choice for plastic-to-plastic joints.

Once details begin to accumulate these ships get difficult to handle. The fixture shown in Fig. 3 may preserve your sanity as well as your work. Slot- ted holes outside the ballast area on the waterline plate are cut before as- sembly. Later these holes can also help mount the model for display.

Step 1. Initial construction. Begin construction by assembling the hull and waterline plate. I use the metal ballast provided in the kit to make the model more stable. Fill and sand the resulting seam as well as any sink holes or ejector-pin marks. Add the kit's gun tubs, depth charges, and aft superstructure without changes (**A**).

Remove the molded coaming from the searchlight platform, part 14 (**B**); it will be replaced with two-bar railing. Assemble the funnels and remove the small ventilator stacks on the aft funnel (**C**); these will be replaced with wire details. Sand the funnel caps flat on top, preserving the separation between the uptakes, then drill out and carve the openings to the proper shape (**D**). Using a razor saw, remove the molded-in bridge windows on part 23, but preserve the locating pins. The photograph shows part 23 in place (**E**); photoetched ladder parts will be added later to simulate window frames.

Remove the molded-on anchor chain with a chisel-point blade and sandpaper (**F**). (I didn't do this until later, but it's best accomplished at this stage.) Apply masking tape as a guide for alignment and mark portholes in the hull and superstructure. Punch the centers with a compass point and drill out the holes using a No. 70 bit (**G**).

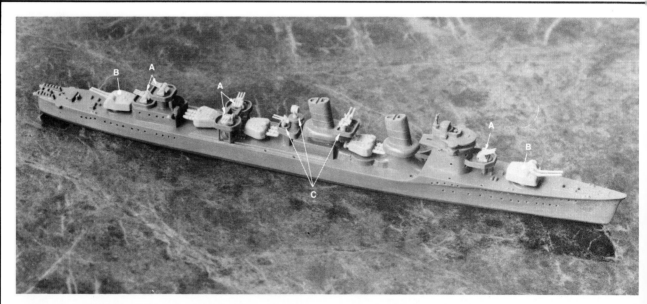

Step 2. Inboard parts and details. This phase is where the inside-to-out process starts. Assemble five Skywave triple 25 mm AA mounts and add these to the proper tubs (**A**). Use the Skywave torpedo mounts and 5″ turrets that are most like those supplied in the kit; add a 1/16″-thick spacer to raise them off of the deck. Shorten the Skywave 5″ gun barrels to a more realistic length and install them in the turrets (**B**). The spacers eliminate the locating pins, so center and glue the turrets and torpedo mounts in place. Mount the Skywave searchlight and twin 13 mm AA guns to the tubs around the after funnel (**C**). These gun tubs are small, which makes for a tight squeeze with the twin AA mounts.

Add hatches to the torpedo mounts and deck structures (**D**). Make these from Evergreen strip plastic (.010″ x .030″) about 3/32″ long. Cut a strip about three times longer than required, then make a shallow cut at the desired hatch length and bend the strip at the cut without separating the parts. Use the extra length as a tweezer handle; remove it after the hatch is set in place.

Add two-bar railing from the cruiser/destroyer set to the after cabin, bridge platform, and searchlight plat-

Step 3. Outboard parts and details. Note that there are two types of davits, braced and unbraced; use the appropriate replacement parts for each type (**A**). Add an .040″ x .040″ styrene spacer across the bottom of the braced davits (**B**) to avoid interference with the torpedo reload boxes, and cut small gaps in the torpedo trolley track to clear these spacers. Measure the distance between the boat mount points with dividers and duplicate this when mounting the davits to the deck. I moved the port-side braced davits aft to clear the forward torpedo mount. If you plan to replace the boat mounting stem on the davits with wire or etched pulleys, do so before mounting the davits on the deck.

Install the single pedestal mount 25 mm and 13 mm AA guns on deck by touching a drop of liquid cement over a positioning mark and placing the part with tweezers (**C**). I located these weapons in the same spots on both port and starboard sides; all single mounts are 25 mm except those next to the bridge, which are 13 mm.

Drill out the hawser and chain holes. Cement the end of a GMM chain in the hawser hole, then loop it behind the capstan and glue into the chain hole. Assemble the small, stockless anchors from the GMM set, bend the shanks, and glue the anchors in holes drilled in the hull at the anchor positions (**D**).

Bend GMM railing to match the curve of the forecastle

form, leaving an access gap in the latter (**E**). It's important to install bridge railings before the mast components. Position photoetched ladders on both sides of the forward gun tub, the lower level of the light platform, one side of the upper level at the gap, the front leg of the tripod mast, the front face of the aft cabin, and the aft upper gun mount (**F**). Fold depth-charge racks and inclined ladders according to the instructions and place them in position (**G**).

I use modified photoetched parts and wire to make additional details. Cut the large vent stacks on the funnel

sides from wire, bend them slightly at the top, and mount them with super glue. Use cut-down photoetched railings, leaving a bit of stanchion as mounting stems for use as small stacks on the front of the funnels (**H**). Hold the part in a piece of masking tape while cutting it.

Bend three pieces of small ladder to match the shape of the opened-up bridge and wings and install these before gluing down the bridge overhead (**I**). Add the lower mast elements and vent stack (**J**). I drilled holes in the sides of the turrets and torpedo shields to simulate apertures (**K**) and filled the davit locator holes (**L**).

deck and measure the length of straight railing to be installed on the main deck (**E**). Attach the photoetched railings using super glue, taking care to avoid excess glue which will granulate when set and become troublesome. The joint at the edge of the deck may need to be sanded lightly.

Additional details include a three-piece jackstay and two-piece forestay made from stretched sprue (**F**) The jackstay should rake aft slightly. Add rudders to the replacement boats by attaching oversize .010″ styrene perpendicular to the stern and trimming it to shape. Place four oars from the cruiser/destroyer set in each open boat using super glue (**G**) and attach the boats to the pul-

leys on the davits. Carefully glue the upper foremast in place, making sure that the rake matches the angle of the front tripod leg (**H**). Substitute Skywave radar antenna and horns for the kit parts (**I**). I use fine copper wire (a single strand from light multi-strand model railroad wire is perfect) for rigging (**J**); this wire is light enough to be pulled straight without putting a lot of tension on the masts.

Step 4. Painting and final details. Spray the entire ship with a one-to-one mixture of Model Master Medium Gray (FS 35237) and Gunship Gray (FS 36118). Since the boats are added before painting, be careful to paint behind them. Paint the funnel caps, anchor and chain, and all AA guns, excluding the mounts, with Tamiya Acrylic Flat black (**A**). Detail the interiors of the open boats, canvas covers on the closed boats, and canvas covers on the turrets with Tamiya Sky Gray (**B**). Mask the waterline with Scotch tape and paint it Tamiya Hull Red (**C**). Cut flags from brass foil, bend into flowing curves, and mount with super glue (**D**). I paint them after they're in place to prevent paint from flaking off.

I've waited for 1/700 scale naval figures and used two of the GMM sets. Bend the brass figures to different positions and thicken them with paint. Add final details before removing them from their frames and use white glue to attach them to the deck (**E**). These add a real finishing touch to a ship model, particularly when action photos or dioramas are planned.

While I did spend about $30.00 on parts to spruce up a $4.00 kit, I have lots of parts left over for use on other projects. Construction time was a whopping 30 hours. Only you can determine if this type of project fits your budget and time limits. Personally, I'm hooked. **FSM**

REFERENCES

● Dull, Paul S., *A Battle History of the Imperial Japanese Navy (1941-1945)*, Naval Institute Press, Annapolis, Maryland, 1978
● Humble, Richard, *The Japanese High Seas Fleet*, Ballantine Books, New York, 1974
● Jentschura, Jung and Mickel, *Warships of the Imperial Japanese Navy, 1869-1945*, Naval Institute Press, Annapolis, Maryland, 1978
● Perry, Loren, *Photoetching for the Plastic Ship Modeler*, Gold Medal Models, Garden Grove, California, 1987

SOURCES

● Skywave kits: Distributed by Empire Pacific Ltd., 10805 East Artesia Boulevard, Cerritos, CA 90701, and Sentai Distributors International, 8735 Shirley Avenue, Northridge, CA 91324
The following are sources of photoetched detail parts:
● The Floating Drydock, c/o General Delivery, Kresgeville, PA 18333
● Gold Medal Models, 12332 Chapman Avenue, No. 81, Garden Grove, CA 92640
● IPMS/USA, P. O. Box 6369, Lincoln, NE 68506
● Model Technologies, 13472 5th St., Suite 12, Chino, CA 91710
● Tom's Modelworks, 1050 Cranberry Drive, Cupertino, CA 95014
● Verlinden, Letterman & Stok, Inc., Lone Star Industrial Park, 811 Lone Star Drive, O'Fallon, MO 63366

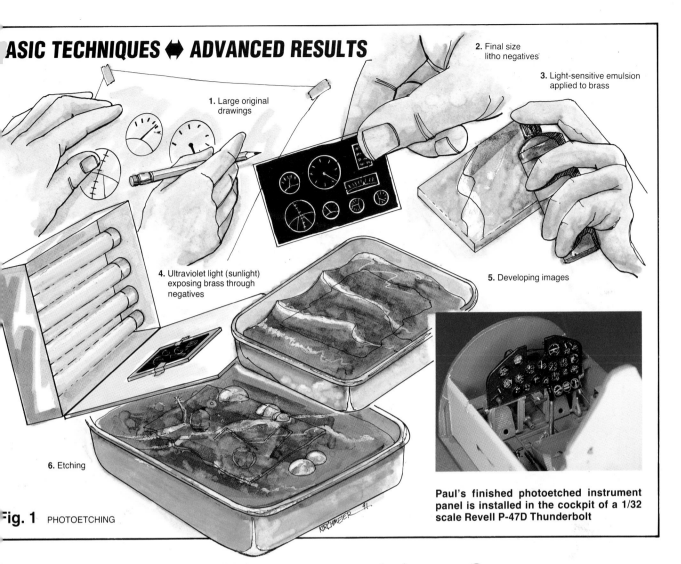

1. Large original drawings

2. Final size litho negatives

3. Light-sensitive emulsion applied to brass

4. Ultraviolet light (sunlight) exposing brass through negatives

5. Developing images

6. Etching

Fig. 1 PHOTOETCHING

Paul's finished photoetched instrument panel is installed in the cockpit of a 1/32 scale Revell P-47D Thunderbolt

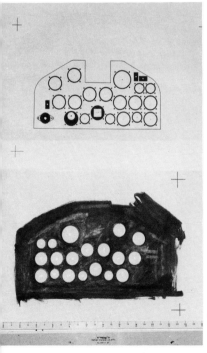

Fig. 2. The large artwork for the front (top) and back of the instrument panel features register marks that will help align the negatives when exposing the brass.

Photoetching for modelers

Creating a bas-relief instrument panel at home

BY PAUL BUDZIK

DESPITE THE FLOOD of photo-etched detail parts for aircraft, armor, cars, and ships, you may find a need for parts that aren't available. Just gazing at those aftermarket parts could make you think it's a complicated and expensive manufacturing process only engineers in white coats can comprehend. Not so. Photoetching is a relatively simple process, one that does involve special materials, techniques, patience, and care. Although my techniques should not be considered the gospel of photoetching, they work for me and others who have tried them.

What is photoetching? Photoetching is essentially a chemical-milling process — it's used to make electronic "printed" circuit boards. As its name suggests, it is a photographic process, too. The desired designs are photographically imprinted on light-sensitized metal, which is then developed. This developed image protects the metal underneath, while the etching chemical eats away unprotected material. Figure 1 is an overview of the process, and you can follow it as you read along.

Original image. The example we'll use is a bas-relief instrument panel for a Revell 1/32 scale P-47 Thunderbolt. Although I wanted raised instrument bezels and rivets, I also wanted holes etched through for the instrument faces that would be added later. To make a bas-relief instrument panel, I needed to create correctly sized images of the face and back sides of the panel. The first

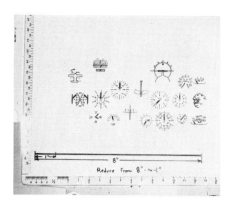

Fig. 3. The instrument faces were also drawn. Here, everything black will appear white on the finished panel.

Fig. 5. The negative/brass sandwich is clamped between two sheets of glass. Once one side of the brass is exposed, simply flip the set over and expose the other side.

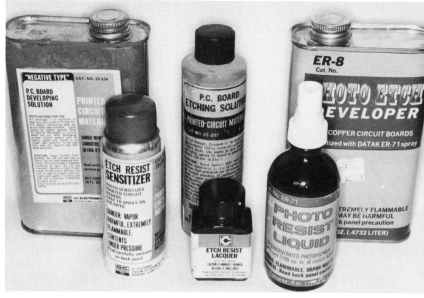

Fig. 4. The group of chemicals on the left is made by GC Electronics, while the group on the right is made by Datak Corporation. In the center rear is a bottle of ferric chloride etchant. Front and center is resist lacquer, which can be brushed onto areas of the metal that need to be protected from the etchant. All these chemicals can be purchased at an electronics supply store.

step is a set of enlarged ink drawings.

Since this process involves a photographic negative, you must make positive images with black ink on good-quality vellum, a frosty, translucent drawing paper. You need to visualize the process before starting to draw: In the negative process, everything drawn with black ink is retained on the final part. (Some photoetching processes use a positive to create the image, but I prefer the negative process.)

One advantage of this system is that you can draw the original larger than the final image. I usually draw my originals eight times larger (8x); this makes it easy to draw fine details. One caution, though: When you produce the original image, you must remember that the weight (or thickness) of the line you use also decreases as you reduce the drawing to the final size. When I draw the 8x original, I never use a line thinner than this:

━━━━━━━━━

Anything thinner could disappear after the drawing is photographically reduced and the brass is chemically etched. You can draw to any ratio that you like, but it's a good idea to always draw to the same enlarged size so you

get a feel for how heavy your lines should be.

Let's go back to the instrument panel. After the original artwork for the front side is drawn, place register marks outside the panel area. These marks can be simple corners or intersecting lines, Fig. 2. Now flip the original drawing face down and tape a new sheet of vellum to the back. You should be able to see the front panel drawing clearly through both sheets of paper. Draw register marks on the new sheet *exactly* over the marks on the first.

Now draw the back side of the panel by following the lines of the front panel underneath. (Remember, if you're working with the negative process, everything you draw with black ink is protected during etching.) In this case, the entire panel is black except the circles for the instruments, which will be etched through. When you're done, separate the two drawings.

A third drawing is for the instrument faces. Tape another sheet of vellum to the instrument panel face drawing and draw the instruments, Fig. 3. Thinking in the negative again, everything you draw with ink will become white on the finished panel — more on this later. You won't need register marks on this drawing.

High-contrast negative. Making negatives is the only step most modelers can't do at home. You need to have high-contrast "litho" negatives made from the original artwork, and your artwork must be reduced to the same size as the final metal parts. Check the telephone book for "lithographers" or "lithographic services." Explain what

you are doing and they will know what you need. You'll be charged by the size of the film provided.

If you have drawn the artwork eight times larger than the final parts, have it reduced to 12.5 percent. Four-times larger (4x) artwork needs to be reduced to 25 percent, and so forth. Make sure the service you use can reduce your artwork to the size you need: Some litho cameras reduce only to 25 percent.

Have all three drawings shot at the same time to eliminate reduction errors. Make sure that the register marks appear in the negatives.

Photo-sensitizing the metal. Just as photographic film is plastic with a light-sensitive emulsion applied to one side, the sheet brass needs a light-sensitive emulsion applied.

K&S sheet brass is available in most well-stocked hobby shops. I cut what I need from the 4" x 10" sheets of .005"-.010"-, and .015"-thick brass. The thicker brass is best for bas-relief etching. Clean the brass with fine sandpaper or pumice and wipe it with alcohol or lacquer thinner.

All the chemicals used in photo etching (photo resist, developer, and etchant) are available in electronic supply stores, Fig. 4. The chemical that forms the light-sensitive emulsion is called photo resist. Depending on the brand you buy, it can be applied as a dip or a spray. I prefer Datak's pump-bottle spray. Since the vapors from photo resist are harmful, wear a respirator mask and make sure your work area has plenty of ventilation.

Apply two heavy coats with the metal laid flat so the chemical settles

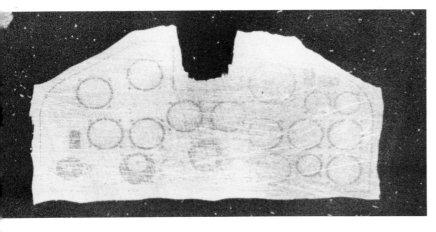

Fig. 6. The developed image can barely be seen on the brass sheet. Paul used black lacquer to reduce the amount of metal to be etched.

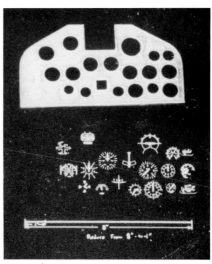

Fig. 8. The instrument negative is placed behind the finished brass panel. Painting the back side of the negative white produces a white-on-black look when the negative is viewed from the front.

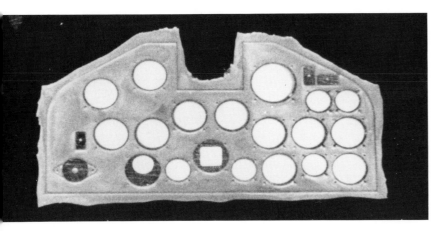

Fig. 7. The instrument panel as it appears after etching. Note the raised bezels around the holes for the instruments.

venly over the surface. Since the chemical is light-sensitive, apply it under subdued light. Total darkness isn't necessary; just be aware that ultraviolet light (there's a lot in sunlight) "exposes" the emulsion. The emulsion takes up to 24 hours to dry (per side), so put the coated brass in a light-tight container while it dries.

Exposing the image. Now you must expose the sensitized brass sheet with the negatives and a strong ultraviolet light source. Sunlight is the handiest source, but grow lights or ultraviolet bulbs work, too. Tape the face panel and back panel negatives together at the top, emulsion (dull side) to emulsion with the register marks lined up. In subdued light, slip the brass in between the negatives and insert this sandwich between two pieces of glass. Clamp the glass together, Fig. 5, and expose the brass to sunlight for two to five minutes per side, according to the instructions on the photo resist label.

Developing the image. After exposure, return to subdued light and remove the brass sheet from behind the negatives. To develop the image, mix developer and water according to the instructions and pour enough to cover

the brass sheet into a print developing tray (available from photographic supply stores) or a glass jar. To keep fresh developer in contact with the sensitized plate, you need to agitate (stir) the liquid every 30 seconds or so. Lifting and lowering one side of the tray about half an inch create enough wave action in the solution. Development time varies with the brand, but it usually takes two to five minutes. Stop development by rinsing the brass thoroughly with water, then let it dry.

Inspect the developed image. Some brands of developer turn the image blue or green; the Datak brand I prefer leaves a transparent but shiny image you can see by holding the sheet at a certain angle, Fig. 6. The rest of the process can be accomplished under ordinary room lighting.

Chemical etching. Brass etching is done with a warm (100 to 125 degrees Fahrenheit) ferric chloride solution. The solution is strong stuff, so wear chemical-resistant gloves. Pour the etchant in a photo tray or jar. Holding the brass sheet with a spring clothespin, place the metal in the etchant. With agitation, etching time is about 15 minutes.

Since the etchant is working from both sides of the brass, you need to leave the panel in only long enough to eat through halfway. If I start with .010″-thick brass, an image exposed on both sides of the brass will be etched all the way through — .005″ from the front side, .005″ from the back.

Monitor the etching process carefully. When the etchant has cut through the holes for the instruments, it's done, Fig. 7. Rinse the brass with tap water to stop the etching and dry with a towel. Remaining photo resist and protectant can be removed by soaking the brass in lacquer thinner and scrubbing with a wire brush.

Remember that third negative with the instrument faces? Paint the emulsion (dull) side with white paint and set it aside to dry. Flip it over and you'll see black instrument faces with white arrows and indexes, Fig. 8. After you've painted the brass instrument panel black, slip the instrument negative behind the panel and align the faces with their respective holes. The finished product looks so real you could swear that the dials are working. **FSM**

REFERENCES

● Kodak information pamphlets No. G-184, *Photofabrication with Kodak resists,* and No. G-185, *Characteristics of Kodak Photoresists,* Eastman Kodak Company, Dept. 454, 343 State St., Rochester, NY 14651

SOURCES

● Photo resist and chemicals: Datak Corporation, North Bergen, NJ 07047 GC Electronics, Division of Hydrometals Inc., Rockford, IL 61101
● Brass sheet: K&S Engineering, 6917 W. 59th, Chicago, IL 60638

Modeling slings straps, and buckles

Easy techniques for adding details and equipment to figures

Straps improve the weapons of both the 100 mm Americ. tanker (above) and the 54 mm British soldier (left).

BY HILBER H. GRAF

DETAILED shoulder slings, straps, and buckles add realism to miniature weapons and enhance the appearance of figures or dioramas. Unfortunately, stock products often omit such details or they are poorly molded. I use inexpensive and easy methods to remedy this problem.

These methods can be applied to make straps for duffel bags, rucksacks, backpacks, and pistol belts. With simple materials and a little imagination, you can add a museum-quality touch to your figures and dioramas.

Foiled again. Lead foil is the best material I've found for fashioning rifle slings. It's pliable, easy to cut with a sha knife or scissors, and can be burnished to a thin scale thic ness. You can buy lead foil in small sheets, but a free sour is the protective lead foil around wine bottle necks. A friends to save this foil for you and you'll soon acqui enough material for dozens of modeling projects. Each pie is approximately 2″ x 3″ and can produce several straps slings.

Use a sharp knife to slice the foil from the wine bott without tearing it. Wrinkles in the foil can be smoothed o by gently burnishing it on a hard flat surface with the ha dle of a round paintbrush.

Rings and buckles. Before starting construction, decide on the style and size of strap required. Cut the foil into strips with a new knife blade and metal-edged ruler (**A**). I make slide rings and buckles from thin wire. For 54 mm scale, lamp cord wire (sold by the foot at home improvement stores) is an excellent and inexpensive material for detailing. After stripping away the plastic insulation you'll find several dozen fine copper wires which are strong and pliable (**B**). You can also use this for spark plug wires, brake lines, antenna wires, and a multitude of other detailing applications.

Shape the wire using pieces of plastic, wood, or other wire as formers: rectangular strips of plastic for buckles; half-round wood dowels for D rings; rod for rings. Simply wrap the copper wire tightly around the form, then slide the ring off and trim away excess wire with a knife or small scissors (**C**). For larger scales, such as 200 mm, I use

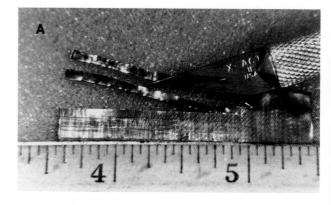

Westrim Crafts' 22-gauge florist wire although it's harder to bend than copper.

Simple slings. I use this simple method to produce a satisfactory sling in 54 mm scale. If a particular type of buckle or shoulder sling is crucial to your project, alter these instructions accordingly (**A**).

Determine the length of the carrying strap you require, and slice two equal-length foil strips to that length. Make three identical copper slide rings slightly wider than the straps. Cut one strap about one-fifth as long as the other strap, saving the excess foil for later. The length of this short strap is varied depending on the appearance desired.

Feed the short strap's ends through two slide rings, bending over enough strap to hold each ring in place (**B**). Secure the contact points with super glue. Feed one end of the longer strap through a ring in the previous subassembly, again bending over just enough foil to secure it with glue. Then feed the opposite end of the long strap through the remaining slide ring (**C**). Adjust the length of the sling by the amount of foil strap you pull through the third ring. Bend the strap back and secure the ring with a drop of super glue.

Now fold the extra length of foil that you cut off around the sling as a slide adjustment clip to keep the threaded long strap end in place (**D**). Trim off excess foil from the slide clip, (**E**) and the completed sling is ready to be attached with super glue (**F**).

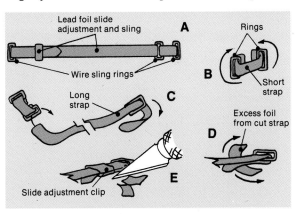

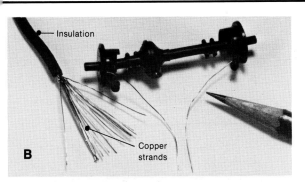

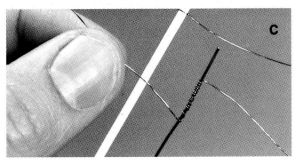

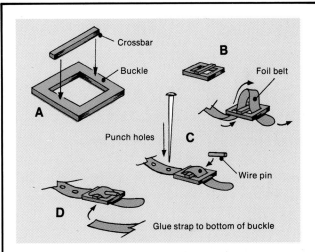

Details in larger scales. Figures 90 mm and larger demand more visible details. Sling fittings and buckles should look like they work. For 1/12 and 1/9 scales, I simulate slide rings using 22-gauge florist wire and make buckles from thin file card or Evergreen .020″ sheet plastic.

Cut a rectangle or square, depending on the type of buckle desired, out of file card or sheet plastic. This buckle should be wider than the strap or belt it will fit on. Cut out the center of the buckle, making certain the opening matches the strap's width. Then glue a narrow crossbar across the buckle (**A**).

Feed a foil belt through the buckle, looping it over the crossbar, and secure it with a drop of super glue (**B**). Use a straight pin to punch several holes in the strap at regular intervals. A wire pin glued to the buckle represents the securing prong (**C**). Your strap or belt could have two or more prongs, depending on the style.

Determine the length of the sling or belt at this point. A second strap, or the opposite end of the first strap, is adjusted to the desired length and glued to the bottom of the buckle (**D**), and you're done.   **FSM**

SOURCES

● Evergreen Scale Models, 12808 N. E. 125th Way, Kirkland, WA 98034
● 22-gauge florist wire: Western Trimming Corp., Chatsworth, CA 91311

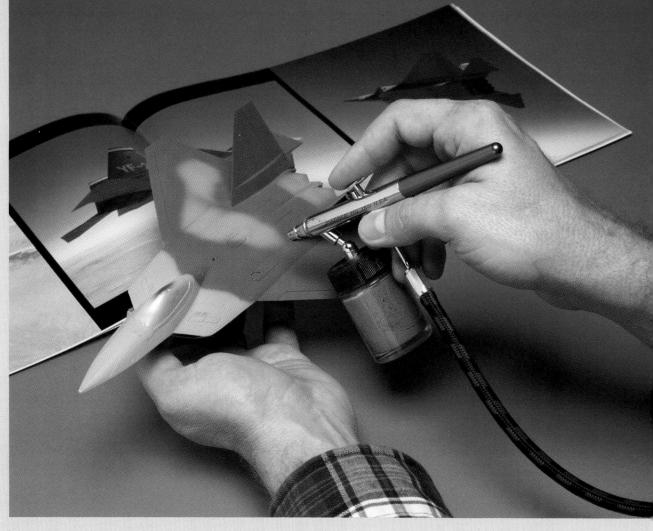

Considered by some to be a tool of the expert, the airbrush is easy to use — once you get the hang of it. FSM senior editor Paul Boyer applies a two-tone camouflage to a 1/72 scale Testor/Italeri YF-22. FSM photos by Chris Becker and A. L. Schmidt.

BASIC TECHNIQUES ◆ ADVANCED RESULTS

Airbrush tips from the experts

FSM authors reveal their airbrushing secrets

BY PAUL BOYER

WHY IS AIRBRUSHING so difficult for some modelers? A few modelers can use an airbrush perfectly the first time, and they may never have trouble. Others can never use an airbrush properly, and they give up. Most of us were frustrated initially, but we experimented with the controls and the thinning ratios and practiced until the tool performed the way that we hoped it would.

I never stop learning about the airbrush. I've been airbrushing models since 1968 and I'm still experimenting. Even so, the lessons I've learned I put into practice, and the more I use my airbrush, the fewer problems I have with it.

So what lessons have you learned? Are you one of the frustrated? Maybe you're one of the few who find airbrushing easy and don't understand what all the fuss is about.

Who are the experts? Nearly all "professional" airbrushers — artists, graphic illustrators, and photo retouchers — paint something other than models. Only experienced modelers can be considered experts on airbrushing models with enamels, acrylics, or lacquers. I chose a baker's dozen of "airbrushing experts" from FSM's authors and asked them to list the type of airbrushes, paints, and air sources they use, as we[ll] as to reveal techniques they find wo[rk] especially well.

Let's go alphabetically, starting with[

Yours truly. I still use the first ai[r]brush I bought, a Paasche H with a N[o.] 1 (fine) tip. I also use a Badger 150 do[u]ble action, Badger 350 single actio[n,] and the new Testor Model Master do[u]ble action in the FSM workshop. O[ur] large compressor here at work feeds a[ir] lines all around the building; at home [I] use a cylinder of compressed carbon d[i]oxide (CO_2).

I've used nearly every model pai[nt] made, but my favorite is still Floqu[il]

th military and railroad colors. I thin
th Floquil Dio-Sol, about two parts
int to one part thinner. When I can, I
y to use Gunze Sangyo Aqueous, Pac-
a Acrylic, and Polly S water-base
ints. They're safer to use than sol-
nt paints such as Floquil or Testor,
t they need special treatment since
ey don't bite into the plastic well. I
in all these acrylics with Polly S air-
ush thinner, which is a water-and-al-
hol mix.

The biggest problem I encountered
hile airbrushing was finding a reli-
le compressed-air source. I started
ith small propellant cans, but long
inting sessions would frost the valve
d reduce the line pressure. In the
ng run cans proved expensive, and I
n't like noisy compressors, so I set-
ed on a compressed CO_2 tank from a
mmercial gas company, Fig. 1. I get
e cylinder filled at a liquor store.
hese cylinders are used in bars to car-
nate mixers and sodas.) The store fills
e cylinders for between $8 and $10. A
ll tank lasts me about a year, or about
0 models. Cylinders are silent and the
gulator can easily adjust the pressure.
owever, the cylinder is heavy and it
as to be refilled occasionally.

All our experts agree with me that
eeping the airbrush clean is critical to
uccessful airbrushing. I clean mine af-
r every spraying session, and some-
mes more than once if I go from dark
lors to light or use a metallic paint.

Paul Budzik. A master modeler and
ng-time FSM author, Paul uses dou-
le-action airbrushes from Iwata, Tha-
er and Chandler, Badger, and Paasche.
or air, he uses a compressor with a stor-
ge tank. Paul likes to use lacquer prim-
rs and Floquil paints thinned with Dio-
ol. He also sprays acrylic enamels,
crylic lacquers, polyurethane clear
ats, and Testor Dullcote.

The biggest airbrushing problem Paul
ncountered was paint drying before it
eached the model's surface. His solu-
ion: Don't spray in 105-degree Fresno,
alifornia, heat! Since he works in his
arage, he avoids airbrushing on hot
ummer afternoons.

Paul always strains his paints to
elp prevent clogging, Fig. 2. He also
ound that high pressure often makes
ry paint grains pile up in corners of
he model.

Hilber Graf. Hilber uses Paasche H
nd Badger 200 airbrushes powered by
diaphragm compressor or propellant
ans (when electricity isn't available).
is favorite paint is Testor Model Mas-
er thinned with Model Master thin-
er. Hilber also likes to use Polly S
ith a 1:1 mix of alcohol and water as
hinner.

Hilber also experienced the problem
f a frosting valve and decreasing pres-
ure with propellant cans; he solved it

Fig. 1. Paul Boyer's favorite air source is this cylinder of compressed CO_2. It can be refilled at commercial-gas supply stores or at beverage-supply services.

Fig. 2. Paul Budzik uses a siphon strainer to keep small clumps of paint from clogging the airbrush and to keep the paint job smooth.

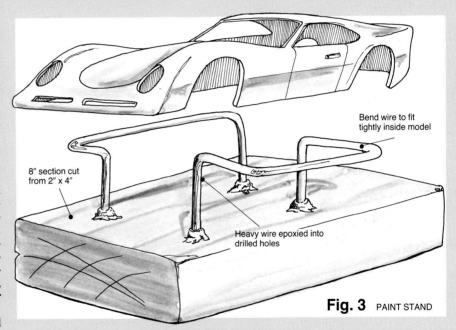

Bend wire to fit
tightly inside model

8" section cut
from 2" x 4"

Heavy wire epoxied into
drilled holes

Fig. 3 PAINT STAND

by immersing the can in warm water while spraying.

Hilber produced a handy gizmo to hold models while airbrushing. It consists of a heavy block of wood with two heavy wire loops, Fig. 3. The loops can be bent to any shape to hold a model firmly from its inside. Now Hilber doesn't have to paint his hand as he holds the model, and fingerprints on fresh paint are no longer a problem.

Tony Greenland. Best known for his marvelous German armor models, Tony uses De Vilbis Super 63 and 63E, as well as Model Master (Aztec) airbrushes. He likes using one of the "silent" compressors, and sprays enamels thinned with mineral spirits. Tony usually sprays at 25 psi, but for fine detail work, he thins the paint further and reduces the pressure to around 15 psi.

Tony knows the value of a clean air-

brush. Cleaning and plenty of practice and patience with the airbrush are his recommendations for success. As far as tricks go, he likes to prepaint the color of markings on his models, then mask the marking color with dry-transfer numbers. After Tony paints the camouflage pattern, he removes the dry-transfer numbers with tape, revealing the marking color, Fig. 4. This way he doesn't have to deal with decals.

Dennis Moore. Prizewinner and FSM author, Dennis uses both a Paasche VL double-action and a Paasche H single-action airbrush. His air supply is a compressor with a holding tank and his favorite paint is the old Pactra enamel thinned with mineral spirits. Dennis also uses Testor Model Master paints and thinner.

Dennis learned to create tight free-hand patterns by practicing on junker

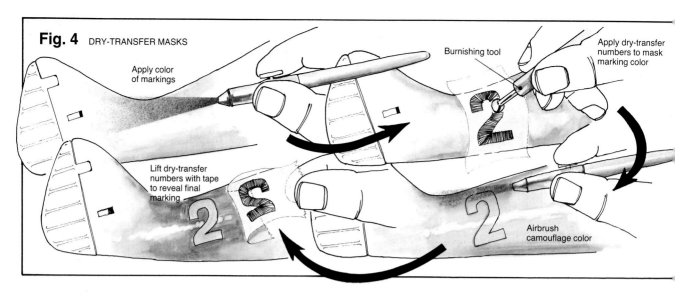

Fig. 4 DRY-TRANSFER MASKS

Apply color of markings

Lift dry-transfer numbers with tape to reveal final marking

Burnishing tool

Apply dry-transfer numbers to mask marking color

Airbrush camouflage color

models. To reduce cleanup time, Dennis never uses the airbrush color cup or bottle. He thins the paint in the original container and dips the airbrush bottle siphon into the paint. Spraying away from the model with the tip open draws a bit of paint into the airbrush. He then sprays the model, and when the paint runs out, he repeats the process. For areas that need only a tiny spritz, Dennis feeds the siphon with a couple of drops of paint transferred with a brush, Fig. 5.

Lewis Pruneau. Lew, who makes BIG models and dioramas, finds the basic X-Acto airbrush powered by a diaphragm compressor adequate for his modeling. He thins Testor Model Master paints with mineral spirits and also uses Humbrol enamels.

Lew hasn't had major difficulties airbrushing, but he does recommend heating the thinned paint by submersing the bottle in hot tap water and keeping the painting room warm — about 80 degrees Fahrenheit. He also wipes his models with a tack cloth before painting, Fig. 6. This sticky, waxy cheesecloth removes dust and sanding residue for a blemish-free paint job.

Bob Rice. A scratchbuilding master, Bob powers his Paasche VL with an Air Pro 1 silent compressor. His favorite paint is Du Pont acrylic lacquer, but he also uses Floquil, Testor Model Master, and Pactra, each thinned with the manufacturer's thinner.

Bob thins his paint more than most modelers, and he's willing to apply several light, almost-dry coats. If paint seeping under masking seems likely, he first airbrushes a coat of clear to seal the mask line. Bob attributes his airbrushing success to cleaning the instrument after every use (see box on page 54).

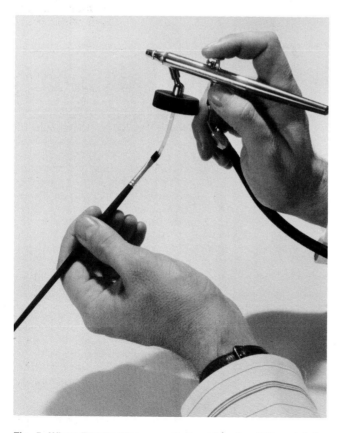

Fig. 5. When Dennis Moore needs to airbrush a little paint, he feeds a drop or two into the siphon with a paintbrush.

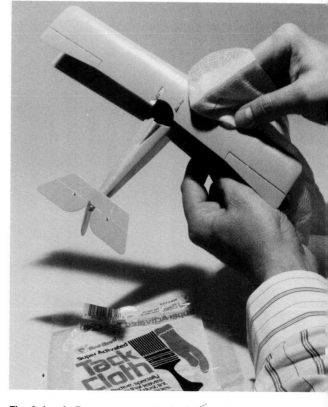

Fig. 6. Lewis Pruneau uses a tack cloth to pick up sanding residue and dust, a key to a smooth airbrush paint job. Tack cloths can be found in hardware stores.

Larry Schramm. Larry uses Paasche H single-action and VL double-action airbrushes, with air coming from a Campbell Hausfeld compressor. Larry's biggest hurdle was painting fine lines. He says a good eye and a steady hand help, but more important is thinning the paint to about 40 percent paint, 60 percent thinner, and cranking the pressure up to 50 psi for fine work. With this formula Larry can spray slightly different colors on fabric-covered ailerons without masking.

Larry prefers Pactra enamels thinned with Dio-Sol for flats, Testor Model Master thinned with mineral spirits for gloss finishes, and Pactra acrylic clear coats. He also uses Floquil paints and Testor Metalizer for his spectacular natural-metal finishes.

When airbrushing a masked line, Larry sprays just enough color to cover. This prevents buildup along the tape line, and when the tape is removed, the line is clean and sharp.

Larry used to have spattering problems with the airbrush, but he found that the old compressor he was using wasn't delivering enough air pressure to atomize the paint properly. He also found that cleaning the airbrush thoroughly helps the airbrush perform at its best.

Stephen "Cookie" Sewell. Armor master Cookie also uses the Paasche H and VL airbrushes. His pet paint-and-thinner combination is Floquil and Dio-Sol. Cookie has been using the same Binks compressor since 1974!

Cookie's favorite techniques include warming his final paint coat bottles (Testor Dullcote or Floquil weathering colors) in hot water before overspraying and using Future floor finish to level his color coats and provide a gloss undercoat for decals.

For a while, Cookie had problems with water condensing in the air line from the compressor. He solved it with an in-line water trap, Fig. 7.

Bob Steinbrunn. This veteran FSM author uses a Paasche VL with a Badger 190-11 compressor and a Norgren pressure gauge/water trap. His favorite paint is Floquil thinned with Dio-Sol.

Bob has found that periodic sharpening of the needle keeps the airbrush at peak performance. He draws the needle tip across a knife-sharpening stone. Bob dusts on three or four light, almost-dry coats of Floquil with moderate air pressure to avoid a pebbly texture and to keep the paint from crazing plastic models.

When spraying camouflage patterns with a tight color demarcation line, Bob thins the paint more than usual so it flows through the airbrush better. With 25 psi, Bob outlines the colored area with a tight spray pattern, spraying toward the center of the colored area, Fig. 8. He then fills the center of the area by opening the tip a little more and using lower pressure to prevent overspray.

Bob solved a spattering problem by thinning the paint more and using higher air pressure plus less paint volume.

David Veres. David builds all sorts of models, but building vacuum-formed aircraft is his strong point. David powers his Paasche V, VL, and H airbrushes with a 1/3-horsepower compressor equipped with a two-gallon storage tank. His favorite paint is Floquil thinned with lacquer thinner, and he also uses Humbrol, Polly S, Tamiya, and Badger Air-Opaque paints.

To produce fine lines, David uses different methods, depending on the type of paint. A 1:1 mix of Humbrol and lacquer thinner sprayed at about 12 psi

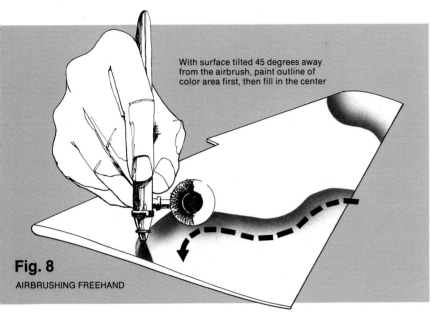

With surface tilted 45 degrees away from the airbrush, paint outline of color area first, then fill in the center

Fig. 8
AIRBRUSHING FREEHAND

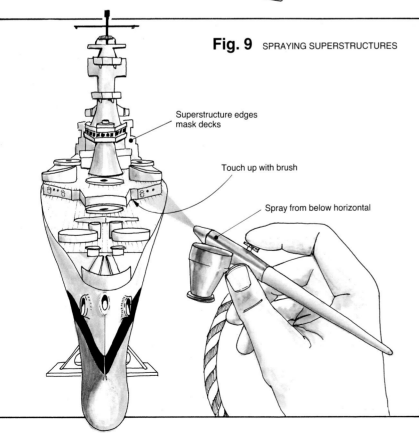

Fig. 9 SPRAYING SUPERSTRUCTURES

Superstructure edges mask decks

Touch up with brush

Spray from below horizontal

produces minimal overspray. He also sprays with the double-action V and VL at 30 to 40 psi. David can spray Polly S with his single-action Paasche H by thinning a color cup full of paint with a couple of drops of Tamiya thinner. The thinner acts as a wetting agent. He sprays this mixture at 45 to 55 psi, and the paint covers quickly since there is little thinner used.

David uses a Paasche VL with a medium tip and needle and a fine cone to achieve the best freehand control with coarse-ground paints such as acrylics. He says air blown through the longer, more tapered fine cone effectively focuses the paint with less overspray.

The biggest problem David overcame was fear of failure. He says airbrushing failures are usually easily fixed. Just paint over most mistakes, and sand off others, but learn from your mistakes.

Rusty White. Painting whiz Rusty White uses a Paasche H airbrush with a W. R. Brown diaphragm compressor. His favorite paint is Testor Model Master thinned 1:1 with Floquil Dio-Sol. This mixture and 21 psi from his compressor work every time. He also uses Dio-Sol to thin all other paints except water-base acrylics.

One of Rusty's favorite airbrushing techniques is spraying the superstructure of ship models using the deck edges as masks, Fig. 9. Slight touch-up with a brush is needed where the structure meets the deck.

Rusty likes to sand each coat of flat paints lightly with a worn piece of 600-grit wet-or-dry sandpaper. He says this makes the paint so smooth you won't need a gloss coat under decals.

Rodney Williams. Rod is known for his high-gloss finishes, and he likes spraying Tamiya acrylics thinned with denatured alcohol through his Badger 200 airbrush. Occasionally he sprays Testor and Floquil thinned with their own thinners. Rod uses a Thomas model 600-13 compressor and sprays between 10 and 25 psi.

For high-gloss finishes, Rod uses multiple light coats. More and more thinner is added to each coat; the final two coats are 100 percent thinner. After spraying flat paints, he sands with 2,000-grit wet-or-dry sandpaper, then polishes the paint with a dry cotton ball, Fig. 10. The surface is so smooth that he can apply decals without a gloss coat. After decaling, Rod sprays a couple of light coats of clear flat with the extra-fine needle in the airbrush.

Getting the best results from your airbrush takes practice. Not all the techniques our experts use will work for you. Eventually, the techniques that do work will become second nature to you, and the airbrush will perform every time you use it. Then you'll be an airbrushing expert too! **FSM**

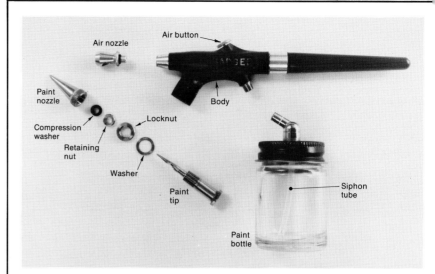

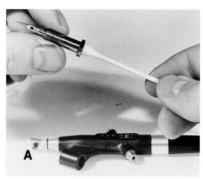

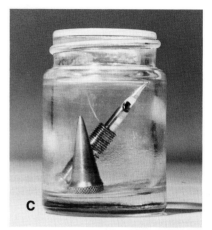

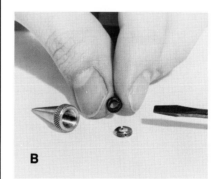

(A) A cotton swab soaked in lacquer thinner can fit into the paint tip and get most of the residual paint. Follow it with a soaked pipe cleaner. **(B)** Before soaking the paint nozzle, remove the compression washer. Lacquer thinner might damage or dissolve the rubber washer. **(C)** To loosen stubborn dried paint, soak the tip and nozzle in lacquer thinner for a few hours.

CLEANING YOUR AIRBRUSH

If you want your airbrush to work properly every time, clean it thoroughly after every session. Most airbrushing problems stem from paint buildup in the tip and siphon, so it's important to make cleaning your airbrush as routine as brushing your teeth.

First, check the maintenance portion of the manual that came with your airbrush. After every painting session, spray clean lacquer thinner through the tip until it removes most of the residual paint. Next, detach the paint bottle or cup and put it aside. Loosen the locknut on the tip and unthread the nozzle from the tip. Use a thinner-soaked cotton swab to bathe the inside and outside of both parts (**A**), followed by a slender, thinner-soaked pipe cleaner. Be careful not to force the pipe cleaner and damage the fragile nozzle.

Hold each part up to a light and look inside — the surfaces should be shiny and clean. If some are still dirty, unscrew the retaining nut inside the paint nozzle and remove the rubber or nylon compression washer (**B**). Soak the metal parts in lacquer thinner for a few hours (**C**), repeat the cleaning process, reinstall the washer, and reassemble.

Check the air nozzle, too. Sometimes paint can splash up into the air nozzle guard and block the tiny hole.

Clean the paint bottle and siphon tube with lacquer thinner and cotton swabs. The pipe cleaner should fit in most siphon tubes. Don't forget the outside of the bottle; spilled paint may get on your hands and then onto the model.

Paul Boyer

The Flakpanzer Coelian (above) was a design only. Tony scratchbuilt the turret on a Tamiya Panther chassis. It sports a dark yellow with green and red-brown scheme. Figure 1 (below) shows a PzKpfw III Ausf N in the overall Panzer Gray scheme.

Painting German tank camouflage

A different approach to armor finishing

BY TONY GREENLAND

W HEN I STARTED modeling six years ago, inexperience and problems with British paints led me to develop my own technique for painting armor models. At that time Compucolor was the most accurate paint available in England, but even after adequate drying time, applying washes frequently lifted and crazed the paint. I also was afraid of applying an overall varnish as there weren't any good ones available. Dealing with these two recurring nightmares is what made me develop a technique that was both safe and pleasing.

I'm sometimes accused of presenting a vehicle that's too "pretty," with only moderate weathering. For this I make no apologies; I'm trying to show the AFV, not the country that it operated in. I try to construct a vehicle as accu-

White highlights

Fig. 2. A StuG 40 Ausf G in dark yellow and red-brown overspray.   **Fig. 4. Note the highlighted raised detail on this PzKpfw IV Ausf D.**

Fig. 5
PAINTING WITH CHALKS
Before
After
Chalk powder

Fig. 3. This SdKfz 232 shows off a dirty winter white scheme, in this case over a Panzer Gray base coat. The white has worn away on the edges, and has streaked.

rately as possible, painted in an appropriate camouflage, and sporting the correct divisional/tactical markings; if I'm pleased with the result then the main requirement has been fulfilled. Those who liberally cover their work with mud often use this as an excuse for poor painting.

The primary difference between my technique and traditional methods is that I rarely use washes. I only use washes of thinned and darkened colors on vehicles that had Zimmerit anti-magnetic coating.

Schemes. Three basic camouflage schemes were applied to German World War Two armor: overall Panzer Gray, 1939-1943, Fig. 1; dark yellow with green and/or red-brown overspray, February 1943-1945, Fig. 2; and winter camouflage, Fig. 3.

I'll describe my technique for applying the dark yellow scheme first. Dark yellow finish frequently had oversprays of green and red-brown. These dark oversprays were issued in a concentrated paste form which was to be thinned when applied by the troops. Different intensities of color resulted depending on the amount of thinning; green could be a light pea green or nearly black if lightly diluted. You don't need to buy individual shades of these greens or red-browns; literally anything goes for these oversprays.

Obviously, the basic dark yellow should be accurate: Humbrol German Pale Yellow (HG7) is a good match, but has a flat finish. I add 20 percent gloss varnish to the paint before airbrushing to give a light satin finish. When a camouflage overspray will be added I sketch the basic scheme before spraying.

Oil paints and dry-brushing. Most modelers give the vehicle a wash of darker earth or black at this point. This is where I start dry-brushing the upper surfaces with the basic yellow enamel. I only use wide (8-10 mm), flat, red-sable brushes; I've never achieved good results with cheaper brushes. The first dry-brushed color provides a base to which subsequent coats will blend.

I mix artist's oil paints (generally white) with the basic yellow enamel. Oils serve two purposes: They blend the light-to-dark areas and ensure the paint on the brush doesn't dry out. Clean the brush with a lacquer thinner if it becomes too stiff; it will dry in seconds. Never dry-brush with a wet brush or one that has any residue of thinner, as doing so will only smear the base paint.

I add increasing amounts of white to the basic color until the last coat is plain white, lightly brushed only on the highest raised detail, Fig. 4. Allow this to dry for 24 to 48 hours.

Chalk weathering. Washes alter the basic color and sometimes the scale effect is completely lost, so I use chalks instead of washes. Use artist's pastel chalks, not weathering chalks which are too greasy; I use mainly black, white, orange, and dark earth. My Faber Castell brand chalks cost about $1.00 per stick and have lasted more than six years. Pastel chalks add a subtlety of coloring that can't be achieved any other way.

File a small pile of black and dark earth (50-50 blend) from the sticks, mix with a 00 sable brush, and liberally

Fig. 7. A slight overspray from the underside onto the side plates helps blend the darker lower portion with the upper colors on this JgdPz 38(t) Hetzer.

Overspray

Rocket tube muzzles

Fig. 6. Black chalk was used on the Nebelwerfer muzzles on this scratchbuilt 15 cm Panzerwerfer 42 auf Sf.

ARMOR SCHEME COLORS

	Topside	Underside	Chalks
Overall Gray scheme	Base - Panzer Gray and black	Base - Panzer Gray and black	Top - dark earth and black; 1 to 1
	Dry brush - gray and white oil	Dry brush - dark earth and white oil	Bottom - black and dark earth; 3 to 1
	Highlight - white oil	Highlight - gray and white oil	
Dark Yellow scheme	Base - pale yellow	Base - dark earth and black	Top - orange and black
	Dry brush - yellow and white oil	Dry brush - dark earth and yellow	Bottom - black and dark earth; 3 to 1
	Highlight - white oil	Highlight - yellow and white oil	
Winter scheme	Base - flat white	Base - gray or dark earth and black	Top - orange and black
	Dry brush - gray or yellow and white oil	Dry brush - gray or dark earth and white oil	Bottom - black and dark earth; 3 to 1
	Highlight - gray or yellow	Highlight - silver	

paint the powder into recesses and bases of raised detail, Fig. 5. Excess powder is simply blown away; where shadows are too strong you can go back and blend using a flat brush. I paint exhausts and muzzle brakes with straight black chalk, Fig. 6. Rust stains are streaked with an orange/black mixture. You'll be amazed at how well the chalks stick, and how well they tolerate handling.

The last step on the upper surfaces is to lightly dry-brush silver on corners and around areas prone to abrasion.

Undersides. I spray the undersides of my vehicles with a mixture of dark earth and black enamel, allowing a slight overspray onto the lower superstructure. All road wheels and tracks are also painted this color. I then dry-

brush, starting with straight dark earth, adding increasing quantities of dark yellow. The last coat again hits only the highest raised detail, this time with a dark yellow/white oil blend.

Paint chalk, now a three-to-one blend of black and dark earth, into all the recesses. It's important to achieve "color sympathy" between the upper and lower hull; there shouldn't be a harsh separation line. The slight overspray from the underside helps achieve this transition, Fig. 7.

Panzer Gray. For vehicles painted overall Panzer Gray I use Humbrol's Panzer Gray (HM4) mixed with 25 per-

cent flat black sprayed on the model. I start dry-brushing with straight Panzer Gray; in this instance I'm actually repainting the whole vehicle by dry-brushing. This has two purposes: It leaves a darker flat finish in recesses where the brush doesn't reach, and it gives a subtle satin finish to the basic paint. The sable brush in effect polishes the paint.

I normally apply decals or dry transfers at this point. Before the gray has dried, I dry-brush Panzer Gray mixed with white oil paint, similar to the method previously described. I continue adding white until I can use

Fig. 8. Tony's techniques bring this Panzerjäger 38 (t) to life. Dry-brushing highlights the edges; chalks darken the recesses.

Dark yellow highlights

straight white without producing sharp contrast, Fig. 8. Then a mixture of orange and black chalk is painted in the recesses and orange chalk rust stains are added.

The undersides are again sprayed a darker shade, but dry-brushed only with a mixture of dark earth and white oil. Underside recesses are painted with a three-to-one blend of black to dark earth chalk.

Winter camouflage. Winter camouflage requires reversing the previous methods, using white as the base color. I spray the entire vehicle flat white, then dry-brush with white oil paint mixed with small amounts of Panzer Gray or dark yellow. Increase the ratio of gray or yellow to white on areas of high abrasion. Corners and high detail are dry-brushed with straight gray or yellow, Fig. 9. Because of the high percentage of oils in these blends, I let the paint dry for several days before going over it with chalks. A blend of three-to-one orange and black, with orange rust stains, is particularly effective.

The underside is painted the same as for a Panzer Gray scheme, but more white is used to achieve the color separation sympathy. Corners, drive wheel teeth, and raised detail can be lightly brushed with silver, but remember to be frugal with metallic finishes.

These techniques can also be used with other schemes, both WWII and modern, and on non-German vehicles. I would recommend that novices try a single-color scheme first. When done well, this simple finish is one of the most attractive.

Don't be conservative with your modeling and don't only "switch on" in your modeling room; try new materials, tools, and techniques, talk with other modelers, and as you travel observe construction equipment and rusting vehicles. Greater authenticity can be achieved by careful observation and application to your models. **FSM**

Fig. 9. Sturmpanzer Brummbär with a winter scheme over dark yellow. Note how the base yellow shows through the whitewash on raised and worn areas.

Photos by Jeff Ollian, drawing by Bob Conners

ob's techniques make it easy to paint road wheels no matter what the size. Here, the ad wheels on a Hetzer get the treatment.

An easy way to paint road wheels

Simple tips to speed up a tedious chore

BY ROBERT SKURDA

I F YOU build armor kits, you've probably spent many hours brush painting tires on road wheels. Here are some techniques that will make painting wheels easier.

You may have to stray from the kit instructions. Most kits call for early assembly and mounting of the wheels. Skip these steps, then build according to the rest of the instructions. Mount the wheels after the model is completely assembled and painted. I usually paint the wheels and tracks just before weathering the finished model.

Cleanup. Detach all wheels from the sprue and remove flash and mold lines. If the wheel has a hole through it, insert a screw in the hole, chuck it in an electric drill or motor tool, and run the wheel lightly against an emery board or nail file, Fig. 1.

Wheels with holes can be skewered like a shish kebab, Fig. 2. Start with wire slightly smaller in diameter than the hole in the wheels and wrap tape around one end of it. Slide on a wheel, a spacer, then another wheel, and so on. Allow enough space between the wheels so you can spray each of them. Tape the end of the wire.

Wheels with holes that don't go all the way through can be sprayed individually or in groups by mounting them on pieces of wire pressed into a piece of plastic foam.

Paint the wheels flat black, then set them aside to dry.

Circle template. I use a circle template to mask off the rubber area while painting the wheel color. This useful tool is available at most art supply stores. When shopping for a circle template, look for one that has holes ranging from $1/16''$ through $1^{1}/_{2}''$ in increments of $1/32''$ or so. Good templates to use include C-thru No. T-800, Timely Nos. T-88 and T-89, and Pickett No. 1204. Prices range from $2.00 to $6.00. However, you might find a bargain if you ask the clerk if he has any defective templates he can discount.

After the black paint has dried completely, carefully remove the wheels from the skewer and place them in a box lid. Place a wheel behind the template and search for the hole that is the closest to the diameter of the inner wheel. To keep overspray from ruining the black outer wheel area, I cover the surrounding holes with tape. With the wheel centered in the hole (I usually clamp the wheel and template together between my fingers and thumb), airbrush the wheel with the overall vehicle color, Fig. 3. Keep the airbrush spray perpendicular to the template and use low air pressure to prevent paint from seeping underneath the template. After the wheels have dried enough to be handled, repeat this process with the other side of each wheel. The circle templates can be cleaned with thinner after the painting session.

If your vehicle is camouflaged, repeat the process for each color. After touching up any overspray with a brush, mount the wheels and begin weathering. I hope that by following these simple steps you'll find painting road wheels a much easier part of your armor modeling. **FSM**

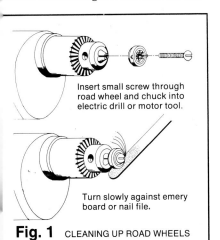

Insert small screw through road wheel and chuck into electric drill or motor tool.

Turn slowly against emery board or nail file.

Fig. 1 CLEANING UP ROAD WHEELS

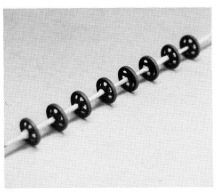

Fig. 2. Road wheels are placed shish kebab-style on a wire. Bob used masking tape wrap as spacers, allowing sufficient room between wheels to ease painting.

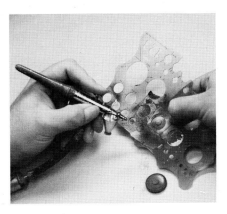

Fig. 3. Here's Bob's circle template technique in action. Note adjacent holes covered with masking tape.

Painting natural-metal finishes

Spray-and-buff metal paints produce realistic bare-metal aircraft models

Monogram's 1/72 scale B-36H Peacemaker is an impressive model — even more impressive when finished with spray-and-buff metal paints. Note the various shades to simulate different metal alloys. (Above right) Larry finishes Monogram's 1/48 scale F-86F Sabre step-by-step. The metallic sheen of spray-and-buff metal paints is one way to beat the realistic bare-metal finish problem. (All photos, FINESCALE MODELER: Paul A. Erler.)

BASIC TECHNIQUES ⬧ ADVANCED RESULTS

BY LARRY SCHRAMM

SEVEN YEARS AGO, Monogram released its 1/72 scale B-36H Peacemaker and I had to include this model in my collection just for its size if nothing else. But halfway through construction, I became sickeningly aware that these birds were mostly unpainted — natural metal. At that point, I had yet to produce a satisfactory natural-metal finish.

There are four ways to produce natural-metal finishes: silver paint, shaded silver lacquers, self-adhesive aluminum foil, and spray-and-buff metal paint. I prefer the last method; it's relatively easy and produces a realistic finish. I've even had people ask if my models were made of aluminum!

Spray-and-buff metal paints are extremely thin and must be airbrushed. After the paint dries for a few minutes, it can be buffed with a soft cloth to a high metallic sheen, simulating bare metal. The major disadvantage to these finishes is their fragility — normal handling and masking can lift the pigments from the plastic. As with any other method of simulating natural metal, flaws in the model's surface will stick out like a sore thumb — your construction, filling, and sanding have to be faultless before you apply metal paints.

The first paints of this type were produced by Liqu-a-plate and Spray 'n' Plate in the late 1970s. Since then Spray 'n' Plate (Advance Products) went out of business and Metalizer and SnJ have appeared. SnJ uses a slightly different approach and says its paints are more resistant to masking and handling. All the current buffing sprays have many colors to simulate different metals; a product list with addresses is on page 45.

Now, let's describe using spray-and-buff metal paints step by step.

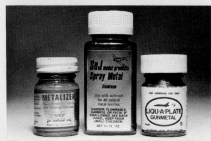

Three brands of spray-and-buff metal paints are available: (left to right) Metalizer, SnJ, and Liqu-a-plate.

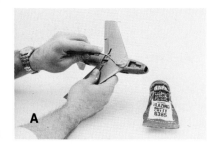  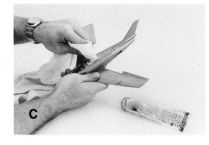

Step 1. Preparation. At first, building a model that will be finished with these paints is like any other kit. I usually prepare the fuselage halves, wings, and drop tanks as subassemblies. Pay particular attention to achieving the smoothest seams possible.

After the subassemblies are completed, start joining them. If you run into fit problems, use auto body filler in the gaps (**A**). I use Napa Glazing Putty because it bites into the plastic and doesn't crack or chip. When the putty is dry, sand it to shape with dry 320-grit wet-or-dry sandpaper. Then wet the sandpaper and lightly sand the surface again. Next, sand with wet 400-grit paper and wipe the model dry with a paper towel.

Since body putty is more absorbent than plastic and will look different when covered with the metal paint, you need to seal it with super glue. Apply a light coat (**B**), making sure that it covers the putty. The glue also fills tiny pinholes in the putty and can be polished glass smooth.

When the super glue is dry, use a fine file to start smoothing the surface. Next, go over all seams with 400-grit sandpaper. I use it dry because it works faster. Follow with wet 600-grit wet-or-dry to eliminate scratches. I attach clear parts with epoxy and carefully sand the joints before painting. Check all seams and sanded areas by holding the model up to a light — if there are any rough areas, repeat all the steps.

Spray-and-buff metal finishes look best when they are applied to glass-smooth plastic. To achieve this smooth surface, I polish the entire model with Blue Magic metal polish, a cream available in auto body supply stores. There's no need to polish areas that will be painted with regular paint, but it doesn't take much longer to polish the whole model.

Apply a small dab of polish to the model and rub it with a soft cloth (**C**). As you rub, the polish will spread out and dry. Further polishing will reveal a beautiful glossy surface — this is what you want. Do a small area at a time and rub the polish in a tight circular motion.

Look carefully for imperfections: pits in the filler, sanding scratches, and so forth. Remember, every blemish will show up under the metalized paint. Since the surface has to be smooth, you won't be able to use a primer to spot imperfections — these paints lose their metallic sheen if applied over paint.

Scrub the model with soapy water and a toothbrush to dislodge polishing compound in corners and panel lines. Let the model dry overnight.

Meet Larry Schramm

Larry began modeling in 1958 when plastic kits started to dominate the hobby. His father helped him build his first model, a 1/72 scale Hawk T-6 Texan. Larry joined the Richard I. Bong IPMS chapter (Milwaukee, Wisconsin) in 1978 and his first prize-winning model was a 1/32 scale F4U-5N Corsair converted from the Revell F4U-1D kit [which will appear in the June 1987 FSM]. His modeling interests include ships, armor, and autos, but aircraft are his favorite. One of his current projects is superdetailing a 1/48 scale Hasegawa F-4E Phantom.

Step 2. Applying spray-and-buff paints. Since these paints will reveal all surface imperfections, they shouldn't be applied over paint. Although you can apply paint over them, most methods of masking are liable to peel the fragile pigment from the plastic. In the case of my example, Monogram's 1/48  scale F-86 Sabre, the yellow and black ID bands were painted on the model first. It's important to paint only the areas that require color — careful masking is in order here. To get the sharpest line, I mask with Scotch Magic Transparent tape.

After the bands dry, carefully mask over them so that the metal paint will come right up to the edge of the bands. Make sure that the painted areas are covered since polishing the metal paint will smear some of its pigments and ruin the paint. The thin Scotch tape is used again so that the buffing rag will slide over it when you polish the metal paint.

I used Liqu-a-plate brand to paint the F-86 and the B-36. First, I sprayed the entire model with aluminum. Be careful to apply a uniform coat; if you get too close the paint will produce splashes that will look strange when buffed.

Let the paint dry for about five minutes. Now comes the fun part. These metal paints are designed to be buffed out, creating a realistic metal sheen. I use a cotton diaper — its size allows me to hold the model in one hand and polish with the other. Both hands are covered by the diaper so I won't mar the finish with fingerprints. Start by lightly rubbing the model until there is a slight sheen to the finish. Now buff faster and apply a little more pressure to bring out more luster and shine. The more buffing you do, the shinier the finish will become. Keep buffing until you get the sheen you're looking for. If you go too far and polish through to the plastic, don't worry! Just re-spray and re-buff.

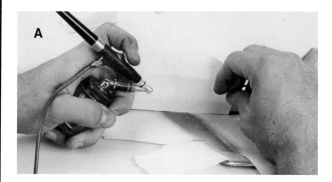

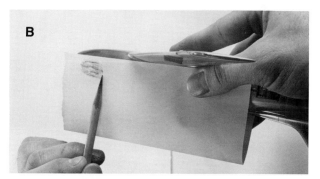

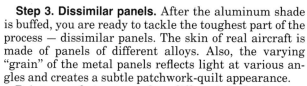

Step 3. Dissimilar panels. After the aluminum shade is buffed, you are ready to tackle the toughest part of the process — dissimilar panels. The skin of real aircraft is made of panels of different alloys. Also, the varying "grain" of the metal panels reflects light at various angles and creates a subtle patchwork-quilt appearance.

Paint manufacturers produce different shades to simulate different alloys. You can create the same effect through buffing. I use several different masking methods. Since the finish is fragile, normal masking tape can't be used. I place a piece of tape on a piece of paper so only about 1/16" of tape is exposed over the edge of the paper. This way, only a small area of tape comes in contact with the metal paint. Treat each edge of the panel this way (**A**); spray the new shade of metal paint.

My second method is to lay a piece of paper over the panel to be painted and rub a pencil on the paper until the outline of the panel underneath appears (**B**). Then I carefully cut 1/16" outside the panel lines and use tape as I did in the first method to hold the mask against the model while I spray on the new shade. If the same shade is used for a number of panels close to each other, they can all be cut from a single sheet of paper (**C**).

The third method is to use sheets of self-adhesive note pad. The adhesive is less sticky than tape and, if gently applied, won't peel the metal paint from the model. Only one edge of each sheet has the adhesive, so one sheet is used for each edge of the panel.

It isn't necessary to keep the stencils in place when you buff, since the minimal bleeding won't be noticeable on adjacent panels. However, by leaving them in place you can buff selected panels to a higher sheen. After the masking is removed, see if the tape has left residue or lifted the paint. Most blemishes can be buffed out.

When you're satisfied with the finish, remove the masking from the painted areas. At this point, handling

the model becomes tricky — the metal paint picks up fingerprints easily. Fingerprints (**D**) can be rubbed out with the buffing cloth. If you get a fingerprint of metal paint on regular paint, it usually can be removed with a pencil eraser. It's best to wear cotton or plastic surgical gloves when handling the product.

Decaling on metal paint calls for special techniques. A clear gloss coat is unnecessary; the finish is smooth and decal silvering won't occur anyway. I don't recommend applying a clear overcoat or sealer on metal paints since this destroys the realistic metal finish. The clear decal film will have the same effect as a clear overcoat, so cut as much away as possible. I've also found that Liqu-a-plate metal paint sometimes cracks underneath decals; this will only be visible under the clear areas. Soak up excess water and setting solution to avoid spots. **FSM**

SOURCES

● Liqu-a-plate: Archer's Products Inc., P.O. Box 9809, Fountain Valley, CA 97728; 8³/₈-oz bottles.
Shade 1 aluminum, 2 steel, 3 titanium, 4 exhaust, 5 bronze, 6 magnesium, 7 gold, 8 gunmetal, sealer.
● Metalizer, The Testor Corporation, 620 Buckbee St., Rockford, IL 61108; ¹/₂-oz. bottles.
Shade 1 aluminum, 2 steel, 3 magnesium, 4 titanium, 5 gunmetal, 6 exhaust, 9 sealer, 12 dark anodonic gray, 13 metallic blue, 14 gold, 15 burnt metal, 16 copper, 17 brass. The following are non-buffing metal paints: 18 aluminum, 20 steel, 21 magnesium, 22 titanium, 23 gunmetal, 24 burnt iron, 25 bright gold, 26 bronze, 27 dark iron, 28 race-car magnesium.
● SnJ Model Products, P. O. Box 28024, Sacramento, CA 95828; One ³/₄-oz bottle plus a ¹/₂-oz bottle of metal powder.
Aluminum, gold, copper, bronze.

Drawing aircraft panel lines with pencil

An alternative to scribing

Rusty White added exciting detail to his Contrail vacuum-formed 1/72 scale XB-70 by drawing the aircraft's panel lines with pencil. (Inset) With an aircraft panel template, you can make quick work of complicated panel lines like these.

Fig. 1. Rusty's technique of accenting exterior detail with pencil-drawn panel lines can improve the appearance of injection-molded kits, too.

BY RUSTY WHITE

WE ALL GO THROUGH differen phases in modeling — that wa my reasoning when I found mysel building vacuum-formed aircraft. I had to happen sooner or later.

After building several aircraft an purchasing several more, it became ob vious to me that few vacuum-forme models provide the quality of panel de tail that I have become accustomed t with injection-molded kits.

To be fair, the way vacuum-forme kits are manufactured one really can expect the fidelity of detail found i most injection-molded kits.

I have read several articles on scrib ing panel lines on aircraft, using every thing from a phonograph needle to a X-acto knife. Regardless of the tool yo use, scribing is a tedious and time-con suming task. When a line is scribe into plastic, ridges are created on eac side of the line by the plastic bein pushed out of the scribed line. Thes ridges must be sanded away. The dus created by sanding settles into th

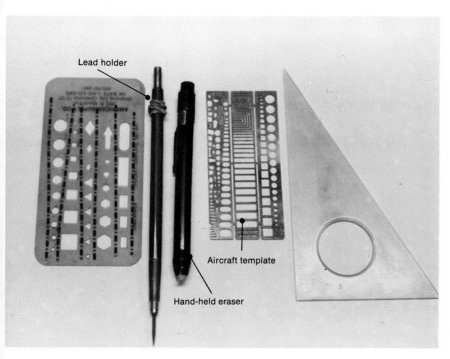

Fig. 2. Here is most of the equipment that you'll need. These tools (except the aircraft template) can be found in architectural and engineering supply stores.

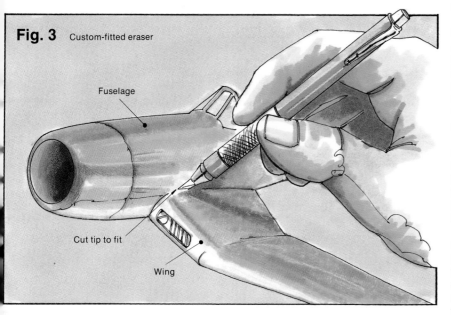

Fig. 3 Custom-fitted eraser

Fuselage

Cut tip to fit

Wing

newly scribed line and must be cleaned out with a toothbrush or similar tool. This method works great for restoring recessed lines sanded away as a result of seam filling, but is impractical for an entire model.

I came across an old FSM article about a modeler who wanted to jazz up an otherwise plain looking F-18 Hornet (FSM Showcase, October 1987). The modeler mentioned that he had sanded away all the panel lines and drew them on with pencil. Although he didn't reveal his method the idea fascinated me. It works for injection-molded kits, Fig. 1. Why not vacuum-formed models?

Tools. Since I am a draftsman, most of the tools I needed were already at my desk. The only tool I had to purchase was a 1/72 scale aircraft panel template, which makes the job easier and faster.

A plastic template with assorted circles, squares, and other shapes in different sizes, and a small plastic triangle will come in handy, too.

The two most important tools you will need are a draftsman's lead holder and hand eraser. The lead holder is a handle that accepts lead inserts, which are sold in several hardnesses. The eraser works like the lead holder, accepting different types of erasers. All of these tools (except the aircraft template) can be found in architectural and engineering supply stores, Fig. 2.

Preparation. I remove the existing panel detail entirely, using 400-grit wet/dry sandpaper, progressing to 600 grit to achieve a smooth finish.

If you just want to accent the existing panel lines, use only 600 grit and sand the entire model, leaving enough detail to guide you when drawing the lines.

After sanding, assemble the model (except landing gear and ordnance) paint it, and apply decals. The model *must* have a *flat* overcoat of paint or the pencil lines will not mark in a smooth, uniform manner. I recommend 2H lead (a medium hardness) so smudging will be kept to a minimum while handling the model.

You will need both hands free. Make a holder out of a shoe box to steady the model while you tape off the lines.

Large panels. Large panels with straight lines are the easiest to produce. To make a long straight line, connect the two ends of the panel with 1/8" draftsman's or graphic tape, leaving a little on each end. Now draw, using the edge of the tape like a ruler. For smooth, continuous lines, avoid lifting the pencil from the line.

Always use a sharp point, and pull the pencil toward you, never push it. Also, as you pull the pencil, twist the pencil at the same time. The twisting keeps the point sharp and uniform on even the longest lines. It may sound difficult, but with practice your models will look like the real thing in no time at all.

Access panels. Access doors come in all shapes and sizes. The aircraft access door template that I use has assorted squares, circles, and other shapes to make any panel, Fig. 2. It's available from Verlinden, Letterman & Stok, Inc., and comes in different scales.

Corrections. One of the advantages of this technique is that if you overrun a line or waver from the leading edge of the tape, corrections are easily and quickly made. Cut the eraser tip to resemble a chisel tip, Fig. 3. This enables you to make precise erasures in even the tightest spots, or to erase an entire line. If the eraser will not fit in a tight spot, trim it to the shape needed. Even after two or three attempts the paint should not be damaged. However, after multiple erasures in the same spot the paint may become glossy. No problem — this will disappear with the final clear coat, which also removes the shine from the graphite lines. **FSM**

SOURCES

● Graphic tape: Chartpak, One River Road, Leeds, MA 01053
● Aircraft templates: Verlinden, Letterman & Stok, Inc., West Port Industrial Park, 804 Fee Fee Road, Maryland Heights, MO 63043

Painting faces in artist's oils

Step-by-step techniques you can apply to any figure in any scale

BY GEORGE DEWOLFE

PAINTING FACES is more interesting — and more important — than any other aspect of figure modeling. The reason is simple: The life and character of the figure radiate from the face. But painting faces isn't easy — for a couple of good reasons. First, human anatomy is extremely complex, even on its surface level, and that complexity is compounded by miniaturization. On top of that, mixing oil colors, then highlighting and shading and blending with them, bedevils modelers into screaming "Uncle" before they are barely off the ground. They needn't, and I hope to show you why.

Before discussing technique I want to emphasize that you can't approach painting faces solely from the standpoint of painting technique. More important than skill with a brush is the earnest desire to create (with paint) the *character* of a real person in miniature. I can't emphasize this enough: If you don't have this desire you'll have a hard time painting figures well, no matter how many techniques you employ. I liken this to the famous children's story, *Pinocchio*, where the toymaker Geppetto wanted to make a wood puppet into a real boy. In painting faces there is a point where, suddenly, the figure seems to leap into reality — I call this phenomenon the "Pinocchio effect."

Breaking the face into planes. It's easier to understand face painting if you first break down the seemingly homogeneous and smoothly contoured human head into planes, Fig. 1. Each plane has a specific type of highlight or shading — for example, the plane of the upper cheek is extremely light compared to the area directly beneath the nose. By understanding the planes you can begin to develop a "feel" for which parts of the face should be light and which should be dark.

Note that the light on this ideal head is from above. Unless there's an awfully good reason to do otherwise, you can assume that the light always come from overhead, like light coming from the "dome" of the open sky. Figure painted this way will be more realisti and natural.

Light from above striking the chiseled planes of the "ideal" face establishes the highlighting and shading pattern to follow when you apply pain to a figure's face. Once you've grasped the concept of the planes, you need make only a minor leap of imaginatio

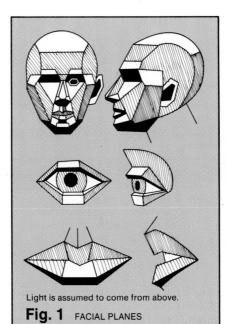

Light is assumed to come from above.

Fig. 1 FACIAL PLANES

Fig. 2. Note how the shading around the eyes, nose, and cheeks of this 100 mm knight provides most of the facial expression and character.

The facial expression is what establishes the character of each of these figures. The author painted all of them with artist's oils using the undercoating, highlighting, shading, and blending techniques described in this article.

from this "plane" face to the normal human head, meanwhile keeping the idea of facial planes intact.

Three kinds of shadows. When light strikes the head it causes three types of shadows. The first kind are on the planes themselves, and where they intersect. These plane shadows are like the dark portions of our sketches showing the head and eye, but they change from head to head. (The differences in these plane shadows are slight between men and women, but considerable between races.)

The second kind of shadow is the wrinkle. These small, but very dark, shadows are independent of the plane shadows and are unique to each figure. They include dimples, the crow's-feet around the eyes, and laugh lines, Fig. 2. The third kind is the local shadow. These are caused neither by facial

planes nor by wrinkles, but by clothing items such as a hat brim casting a deep shadow on the upper forehead.

Keep these three different types of shadows in mind when you paint faces. Usually, you'll want to start with a broad application of paint to render the planes of the face, then concentrate on specific wrinkles, then add local shadows and details.

Brushes and equipment. Every figure modeler has his own favorite tools and paints. Brushes in particular are highly personal pieces of equipment (I know a modeling couple with "his" and "hers" sets of brushes — both locked up separately). Choose your brushes for the quality of the point and for durability, and don't ever use them for anything but figure painting.

I paint faces with Winsor & Newton Series 7 red sable brushes, and I con-

sider them the finest figure painting brushes available. Buy a No. 000 for detailing, a No. 0 for medium work and blending, and a No. 1 or No. 2 for general painting. A Winsor & Newton Series 12 brush is good for blending, and the Series 52 flat shape is good for drybrushing and applying paint to large areas. The Grumbacher No. 7805 Cat's Tongue is also excellent for this purpose. I've also found Teka Fine Line brushes of very high quality.

A binocular magnifier that fits over your head such as the Optivisor is a necessity for painting faces. You will get eyestrain and headaches if you do not use one. I have 2x, 3x, and 4x attachments for mine, Fig. 3.

Almost anything can serve as a pal-

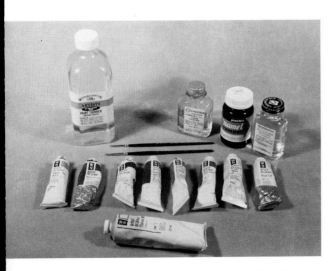

Figs. 3 and 4. (Right) The author's workbench, with a figure in progress. George rates the Optivisor binocular magnifier among his most important tools. (Above) Supplies, clockwise from top, Winsor & Newton thinner, Grumbacher linseed oil, Pactra Namel thinner, Grumbacher Oil Painting Medium No. 1, and Winsor & Newton Artist's Oils.

ette for mixing paints, from newspaper to index cards to glass plates. I use plastic-coated freezer paper because it is inexpensive, clean, and disposable. Round toothpicks are useful for mixing paint, although many painters use a palette knife. You'll also need plenty of tissue paper or rags for wiping and cleaning brushes.

Paint, thinner, and additives. Nothing but the best will suffice for painting faces, and for me that's Winsor & Newton Artist's Oils (the high-quality line,

OILS
Titanium White
Terra Rosa
Burnt Umber
Permanent Magenta (Quinacridone)
Naples Yellow or Jaune Brilliant (I prefer the latter)
Yellow Ochre
Alizarin Crimson
Mars Violet
Mars Red
Mars Orange
Brown Madder Alizarin
Flesh Tint
Payne's Gray

POLLY S COLORS
Desert Pink (basic undercoat flesh color for men)
Cherry Pink (for women)
Dirty White
Night Black
Ogre Dark Brown
Dragon Blue

Fig. 5   COLORS FOR PAINTING FACES

not the London oil colors), Fig. 4. Most other oil paints I have tried have too much oil in them to be useful for painting faces, but figure painters disagree almost violently about paint. One of the best painters I know uses Grumbacher Finest Oils, and most painters use at least a few specific colors from various manufacturers other than their first choice. Winsor & Newton oils, however, seem to be ground finer and blend better than the others. Figure 5 lists the oil colors you'll need for painting faces, as well as several water-base Polly S colors for undercoating and painting eyeballs.

Many painters use pure gum spirits of turpentine as a thinner and brush cleaner for oils, but the smell drives me crazy! I prefer either Pactra 'Namel thinner or Winsor & Newton mineral spirits, which is odorless and available in pint containers at a considerable savings over smaller sizes. A favorite of others is Grumbacher Oil Painting Medium No. 1, which imparts a flat finish to oils, but I find its smell, too, obnoxious.

When used as a painting medium linseed oil renders oils glossy. I use it mainly to slightly moisten and "point" the brush just before blending. Poppy seed oil is generally better for flesh tones as it does not yellow pale colors. Cobalt Drier accelerates the drying of oils — a tiny drop from the point of a toothpick into a pea-sized blob of paint will make it dry in 12 to 18 hours.

Many figure painters use Dorland' Wax Medium to impart a flat finish t oil paint. The proportions vary wit each color, but about one-third Dorland' to two-thirds paint will do for starters Most of the time, mixing thinner wit oils yields an acceptably flat finish, bu you'll have to experiment to see wha works for you.

Priming and undercoating. Primin is an important step in figure paintin The primer reveals flaws in sculptin and assembly and serves as a base fo the undercoat colors. For metal figure it acts as a barrier to prevent oxidatio which causes a white powder known a "lead disease," ruining the figure.

Metal should be primed with eithe Imrie/Risley Primer or Floquil Spra Figure Primer. After this protectiv coat I airbrush the figure with Floqui Primer (RR9) or Floquil Reefer Whit (RR11). Either serves as a "toothe base" (a paint surface rough enough t hold other paint) for the undercoat. airbrush plastic figures with Floqui Reefer White or flat white enamel.

Undercoating simply means layin down a coat of paint without highligh ing or shading, **A** (see box, top of thi page). For the face I use Polly S Deser Pink (PCA810) for men and Cherr Pink (PF22) for women. Polly S won rub off when you add highlights an shadows with oils; enamels such a

D

PAINTING A FACE STEP BY STEP

(A) A Series 77 90 mm pilot after the figure has been primed, then undercoated with Polly S acrylic colors. (B) The eyeballs have been painted, and the flesh areas around them touched up with the Polly S flesh color. (C) The figure after applying the first blend shadow and highlight colors, and (D) after blending them. (E) The second blend shadows and highlights applied, and (F) blended. (G) The face after the finishing blend, with all wrinkles and detail shadows added, and extra color worked in to give the figure life.

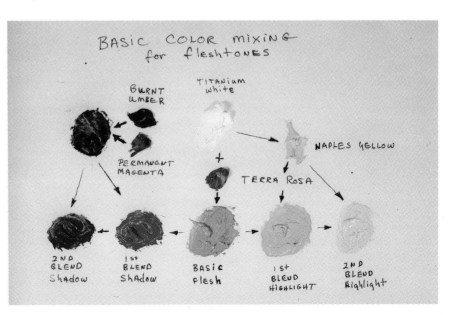

Even these 1/76 scale desert rats show lots of character. The eyes are mere black slits, but the lower eyelids have been suggested with paint to give form to the eyes.

Humbrol and Pactra would wear off during blending.

First: eyeballs. Paint the eyeballs first: Doing so begins to establish the figure's character. Use Polly S so that once the eyeballs are painted on they cannot be changed by accidental smearing. If oil paint happens to cover them during blending, a brush dampened with thinner will remove the errant color and leave the eyeball clean and intact.

Paint the whites of the eyes first with Polly S Dirty White (PCA805), Fig. 6. Next, using either Ogre Dark Brown (1427) or Dragon Blue (1432), add a line covering the middle half of the eye; this will become the iris. Don't worry about the color overlapping the top and bottom eyelids; you'll go over this later. Next add a black line inside the iris to represent the pupil.

Now reduce any of the lines outside the eyeball with the basic Polly S flesh color, outline the inside of the eyelid with dark brown, touch up, and you're done, **B**. It takes practice to get this right, but after just a few figures you'll feel confident. And don't forget to use that binocular magnifier!

Mixing flesh colors in oils. Before you apply oils over the Polly S to establish planes and wrinkles you must learn to mix a basic flesh tone and highlight and shadow tones based on it. This is relatively easy.

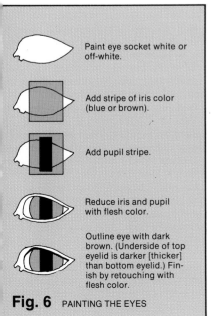

Paint eye socket white or off-white.

Add stripe of iris color (blue or brown).

Add pupil stripe.

Reduce iris and pupil with flesh color.

Outline eye with dark brown. (Underside of top eyelid is darker [thicker] than bottom eyelid.) Finish by retouching with flesh color.

Fig. 6 PAINTING THE EYES

BASIC COLOR MIXING for fleshtones

BURNT UMBER

TITANIUM WHITE

PERMANENT MAGENTA

NAPLES YELLOW

TERRA ROSA

2ND BLEND SHADOW

1st BLEND SHADOW

BASIC FLESH

1st BLEND HIGHLIGHT

2ND BLEND HIGHLIGHT

Fig. 7. Here's how George recommends mixing a basic flesh tone from artist's oils, as well as variations of the basic tone for shading and highlighting.

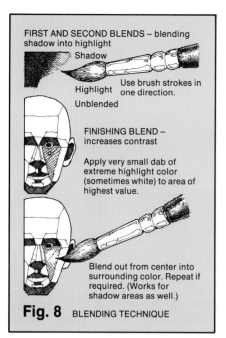

FIRST AND SECOND BLENDS – blending shadow into highlight

Shadow

Highlight — Use brush strokes in one direction.

Unblended

FINISHING BLEND – increases contrast

Apply very small dab of extreme highlight color (sometimes white) to area of highest value.

Blend out from center into surrounding color. Repeat if required. (Works for shadow areas as well.)

Fig. 8 BLENDING TECHNIQUE

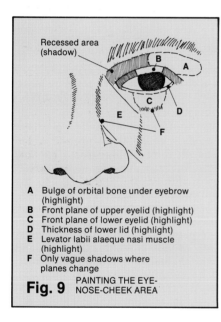

Recessed area (shadow)

A Bulge of orbital bone under eyebrow (highlight)
B Front plane of upper eyelid (highlight)
C Front plane of lower eyelid (highlight)
D Thickness of lower lid (highlight)
E Levator labii alaeque nasi muscle (highlight)
F Only vague shadows where planes change

Fig. 9 PAINTING THE EYE-NOSE-CHEEK AREA

Start by mixing a basic medium flesh tone with terra rose and titanium white, Fig. 7. Use the back of your hand as a reference. Next add more white and a little Naples yellow or Jaune brilliant to make a medium highlight (I call this the first-blend highlight) and more white and Naples yellow for the second-blend highlight.

For the shadow tones, mix equal amounts of burnt umber and magenta and add this to the basic flesh color to obtain a first-blend shadow and a second-blend shadow.

Shading, highlighting, and blending. I break shading and highlighting into three steps: first blend, second blend, and finishing blend. The first blend involves laying in and blending the planes of the face and local shadows. In the second, I paint deep recesses and wrinkles and add contrast. The finishing blend increases contrast, smooths tones between planes, and adds detail and color.

Start by moistening the brush with thinner. Mix thinner into the first blend shadow color until it has the consistency of Polly S, perhaps a little thicker. Experiment to find the consistency that will make the paint flow evenly and smoothly from the brush.

Apply the first-blend shadow color, **C**, covering all medium shadow planes of the face. These include the side of the face, underneath the chin, the sides of the nose, the hairline, and under the lower lip. Leave out detail shadows, and skip the eyes in this step. Use the paint sparingly — a little goes a long way. Next, apply the first-blend highlight to areas that are not covered by the shadow mix. Blend the shadow and highlight colors together.

Moisten the brush with linseed or poppy oil and wipe it off so that the brush is dry but has a distinct point. Smooth the area where the highlight and shadow meet, **D**. Brush delicately, generally in one direction, Fig. 8. If blending in one direction doesn't complete the job, go back and blend the other way. The photos are greatly enlarged to show what you'll see through the magnifier. Without magnification the brush marks and irregularities would be too fine to see.

In the second blend, add contrast with lighter highlights and darker shadows. Add details such as the shape of the eyes and mouth, and general recesses such as the laugh lines around the mouth and nose. Apply the colors and blend them as you did before, **E** and **F**. The figure will come to life.

The finishing blend. This is the most critical phase. Imagine that you are creating the character of a real person. During the finishing blend you will increase the contrast, smooth lines between shadows and highlights, accentuate small details, and add color.

Like the overall process of painting the face, I divide the finishing blend into three steps. They are: (1) creating expression around the eyes, nose and cheeks; (2) adding color to the cheeks and lips; (3) increasing the contrast around the chin, nose, and cheeks. This is also the time to add a five o'clock shadow and put more color in wrinkles.

Start with the eyes, nose, and cheeks. The eyes are indeed the windows to the soul, and they're tricky to paint. Establish the shape of the eye, Fig. 9, with two frontal planes (upper and lower lids), four side planes (two upper, two lower), the highlight on the lower lid, and the shadow under the upper lid. Getting this shape right is critical on figures 54 mm or larger. To avoid bulg-

ing eyes, exaggerate the area immediately around them.

Pay special attention to the highlight areas around the eyes, painting them larger than usual so the planes and features are prominent. Use the paint as it comes from the tube, undiluted with thinner. Apply a speck of off-white paint about the size of the dot on an "i" made with a pen, then blend the speck outward into the small highlight area, for example, the upper eyelid. You may have to repeat this two or three times, and careful observation and evaluation of the effect is crucial.

Next add color to the cheeks and lips. Mix Alizarin crimson with the basic flesh color to get a medium pink. Apply this to the hollows of the cheeks just below the cheekbone and to the lower lip. Use pure Alizarin crimson or magenta for the underside of the upper lip. Work the cheek color into the flesh tones. Add white to the front plane of the lower lip and blend with the pink. You may need to repeat this.

Step 3 involves increasing contrast. At this point, generally speaking, the overall appearance of the face is still flat. Increase the contrast by adding white or off-white (a little Naples Yellow or yellow ochre added to white will do). Add specks of off-white to the tops of the cheeks, bridge of the nose and nostrils, top of the chin, and perhaps underneath the nose just above the lips. Blend the specks outward as before. Examine the figure under low, diffuse illumination (put your back to the light and hold the figure in your shadow). After this step the face should be just about right, **G**.

Sometimes the shadow recesses may seem dull because of too much burnt umber in the shadow mix. Brighten these areas by sparingly adding either Mars orange or Mars red and Brown Madder Alizarin, blending well. The area just under the eyebrows may need a touch of Mars violet — not too much, this color is very powerful. Add a five o'clock shadow by working a little Payne's gray into the shadows around the cheek and mouth.

And now, practice. After five or ten faces you should be well on your way toward proficiency. Then you'll be able to concentrate on the subtle business of changing the character and expression from one face to the next. When you're ready, buy a good book on anatomy such as the one listed below, and study the elusive details and expressions of the human face. And may moss never grow on your paintbrush! **FSM**

REFERENCES

Rubins, David K., *The Human Figure: Anatomy for Artists*, Viking/Penguin, New York, 1975.

Rusty White has devised a crafty (and easy) technique to replicate wood decks for large-scale ships.

BASIC TECHNIQUES ✦ ADVANCED RESULTS

Simulating wood planking with tape

Hands-on deck advice

BY RUSTY WHITE

AS A BIG-SHIP enthusiast, I am intrigued by the radical changes in color from peacetime to war.

A characteristic that most United States vessels shared during World War Two was wood decks. The decks of battleships, cruisers, and carriers were stained blue to elude aerial observers. Some ships had elaborate camouflage patterns to enhance this effect.

After the war, decks were restored to their natural color. So, modeling any peacetime U. S. vessel will involve painting a natural wood deck. While this doesn't present much of a problem in 1/700 scale, 1/400 and larger will require the illusion of individual planks.

I have tried using a thin brush and straightedge, but this is time-consuming and ineffective. I considered painting strips of clear decal film different shades of brown, but touch-up would be a nightmare.

Finally, I found a method that works, can be easily touched up, and doesn't take much time.

Mixing the paint. Earth brown is a good color to start with. You'll need yellow, flat white, red, and black, as well as three clean jars for mixing.

We want three shades of brown. The difference among the shades is slight; mark each jar to avoid confusion.

First, mix a full jar of the lightest shade. Mark it "No. 1." You should end up with about twice as much of this color as the others, because you will need more of it. Now, pour a little of color No. 1 in each of the remaining jars. If you don't have the luxury of a paint shaker, put three or four BBs in the jar to help mix the colors.

Add a few drops of red and black to make the intermediate color. For a richer brown, add a few drops of yellow. Mark this jar "No. 2." For the final and most prevalent shade, repeat the process for No. 2 and add a few more drops of black. Mark this jar "No. 3."

Check often for the desired shade. It is easier to darken a color than it is to lighten it.

Testing colors. Now, test each color on scrap plastic. Spray No. 1 first, then spray an overlapping strip of Nos. 2 and 3. If any of the shades needs adjusting, now is the time.

Painting the deck. Paint the entire deck surface with No. 1. Using 1/32" graphic tape (or thinner tape, depending on your scale), cut varying lengths (1/4"-1 1/2"), Fig. 1. Place them on the deck randomly, running in the direction of the planking, Fig. 2.

Next, *dust* the deck with No. 2. Add more tape strips, then dust using color No. 3, and set aside to dry.

When the paint is dry, remove all the tape. The layered effect is obvious.

For the final step, *dust* the deck with No. 1 until you are satisfied with the overall shade. Don't overdo it; too many coats could result in ridges when the tape is removed.

This technique can be used for Soviet red-stained decks as well as camouflaged decks stained blue. **FSM**

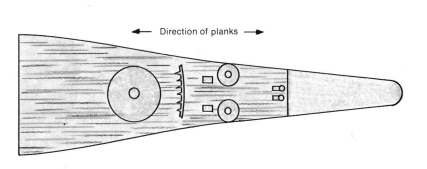

← Direction of planks →

Fig. 1. Graphic tape can be found at art supply stores.

Fig. 2 Color guide Color 1 Color 2 Color 3

A plain-Jane jet plane is transformed to the colorful Korean War mount of future astronaut John Glenn with the decals provided in the Fujimi 1/72 scale F-86 kit.

The delights (and disasters) of decaling

Sometimes the final step toward a beautiful model can trip you

BY PAUL BOYER

WHEN I WAS A KID, my favorite part of building models was applying the decals. (Then, of course, it came only an hour after opening the box.) It's still my favorite step, but now it follows dozens (and sometimes hundreds) of hours of construction, detailing, and painting. As a kid, it didn't matter much that the decals obscured those funny lines and bumps or started to peel off the unpainted plastic. Now I devote lots of time and effort to make sure they conform to surface detail and stay on the model for good.

Next to painting, decaling is the most critical step in finishing a model. At best, any major mistakes can mean replacing the decals at some expense. At worst, you may have to sand off dry decals, probably removing some of the paint job. It's make or break time.

Anatomy of a decal. Decal is short for *decalcomania*, which means a transfer of an image from one surface to another. This includes vinyl labels, dry-transfer rub-ons — even bumper stick-

ers! But for modelers it means those little markings you dip in water and slide onto the model. Water-slide decals are the most common type of markings provided in plastic kits, and that's the type we'll discuss here.

Model decals can be printed a number of different ways. The most common method is silk-screen printing. Some are printed on large letterpress machines, but more and more kit manufacturers are going with offset printing. Offset printing has its advantages: speed and relatively low cost. The full spectrum of colors can be produced using only five colors of ink: white, yellow, red, blue, and black. This is done by printing several layers of tiny colored dots on top of each other. Printing red dots over yellow makes orange, blue on yellow makes green, and so forth.

Unfortunately, these dots may not be acceptable to finicky modelers. Another disadvantage is that offset inks are translucent; they are made to dye paper surfaces and depend on the paper's opacity for color saturation. Light colors such as white and yellow may

have to be run twice to get acceptab[le] opacity, and that may result in p[oor] registration (misaligned images).

On the other hand, silk-screen prin[t]ing uses opaque inks, but each co[lor] has to be printed separately. If th[ere] are three shades of blues in the ma[rk]ings, three passes through the pr[ess] will be needed. That takes time, a[nd] time is money. Silk-screen-printed [de]cals take longer to produce and c[ost] more than offset-printed decals.

Water-slide decals have inks print[ed] on a clear carrier film that links all t[he] colors together when the marking is [re]moved from the backing paper. T[he] clear carrier film can be spot print[ed] (just a little larger than the image) [or] printed over the entire sheet. Sp[ot] printed clear carrier film allows you [to] dip a number of markings at once a[nd] each will float free of the backi[ng] sheet. You'll have to cut each of t[he] markings out if the carrier is over t[he] entire sheet.

Applying decals step by step. O[ne] of the first lessons modelers learn [is] that water-slide decals don't stick

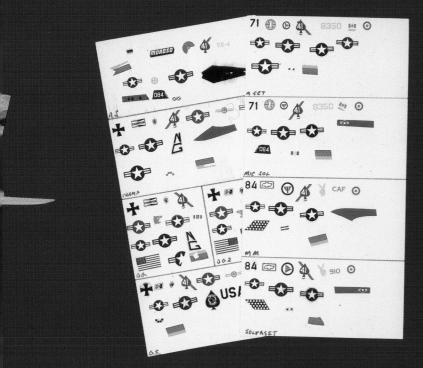

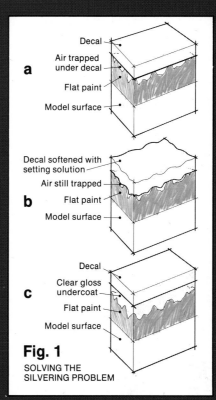

Fig. 1
SOLVING THE
SILVERING PROBLEM

Labels in Fig. 1:

a
- Decal
- Air trapped under decal
- Flat paint
- Model surface

b
- Decal softened with setting solution
- Air still trapped
- Flat paint
- Model surface

c
- Decal
- Clear gloss undercoat
- Flat paint
- Model surface

l 9 decal-setting solutions were tested on 14 decal brands. Grooved Evergreen sheet yrene was used as the test surface.

re plastic. Plastic kit molds are rayed with a release agent to ensure paration of the plastic from the metal olds. Some of this oily substance ings to the plastic and can prevent int and decals from adhering. It's imortant to wash plastic model parts ith soapy water before painting, and cals should be applied to *painted* astic.

Decal paper is coated with a waterluble adhesive that sticks the decal the model. In most cases, this adheve is all you need to do an acceptable cal job, but there are pitfalls in the th. These days, most modeling paints oduce a flat finish. However, it's difcult to get decals to conform and adere to flat paints; they have a rough

texture and keep the decals from snuggling down to their uneven surface, Fig. 1a. To remedy this, modelers use decal-setting solutions which soften the decal and draw it down onto the paint, Fig. 1b. But sometimes, even this isn't enough.

If a decal doesn't conform to the painted surface, it traps air underneath the clear film. Light passes through the film, through the air underneath, bounces off the tiny hills and valleys of the rough paint surface, and goes back up through the air and the film again. When light goes through all these maneuvers it scatters and bends, creating an opalescent or "silver" look. To many modelers, this is unacceptable. The best way to avoid this prob-

lem is to apply decals to a glossy surface.

Glossy paints are smooth and keep air from getting trapped underneath the decal, Fig. 1c. If flat paints are used, a coat or two of clear gloss over them will help decals adhere.

After the glossy finish has dried for 24 hours, you're ready to apply the decals. Some modelers prefer to cut away as much of the clear carrier film as possible; others leave the spot-printed film alone. In either case, carefully cut the decal out of the sheet, Fig. 2. Use light pressure when cutting out the decals. If you press too hard, the paper may curl and crack the fragile inks.

Some decal-setting solution brands recommend applying a few drops on the

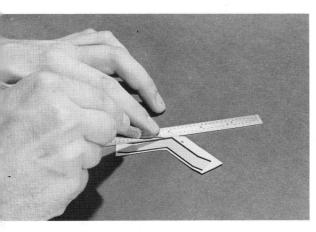

g. 2. Using a sharp blade, lightly cut the clear film from the de- l. Pressing too hard may crack the inks.

Fig. 3. Setting solution applied under the decal will help elimi- nate air bubbles.

Fig. 8

DECAL-SETTING SOLUTIONS

Decal-setting solution Manufacturer, address, and price	AIRFIX	AMT/ERTL	ATP	CARTOGRAPH	DETAIL & SCALE	FUJIMI	HASEGAWA	HELLER	MICROSCALE	MODELDECAL	MONOGRAM	REVELL	SCALE-MASTER	TAMIYA
Accu-Set SMP Products, 63 Hudson Road, P. O. Box 72, Bolton, MA 01740 1 oz, $2.00	X	X	✔	✔	X	✔	✔	—	✔	X	X	✔	✔	✔
Champ Decal-Set Champion Decal Company, Box 1178R, Minot, ND 58702 2 oz, $3.25	X	X	✔	✔	✔	✔	✔	—	X	✔	X	✔	✔	✔
SuperSett D. G. Modelling Products, 8080 Langdon Avenue, Van Nuys, CA 91406 1 oz, $1.29	X	✔	✔	✔	✔	✔	✔	✔	✔	✔	✔	✔	✔	✔
SuperSett Too 1 oz, $1.29	✔	X	✔	✔	✔	✔	✔	—	X	✔	X	✔	✔	✔
Gunze Sangyo Mr. Mark Softer distributed by Marco Polo Import, Inc., 2239 Tyler Avenue, Unit A, South El Monte, CA 91733 40 ml, $1.95	X	X	✔	✔	✔	✔	✔	✔	✔	X	X	✔	✔	—
Microscale Micro Set Krasel Industries, Inc., 919 Sunset Drive, Costa Mesa, CA 92627 1 oz, $1.50	✔	✔	✔	—	✔	✔	✔	✔	✔	X	✔	✔	✔	—
Microscale Micro Sol 1 oz, $1.50	✔	✔	✔	—	✔	✔	✔	✔	✔	X	X	✔	✔	✔
Model Master Decal Set Testor Corporation, 620 Buckbee Street, Rockford, IL 61108 ½ oz, $1.29	✔	✔	✔	—	✔	✔	✔	✔	✔	✔	✔	✔	✔	—
Solvaset Hobsco Inc., 5601 West Florist Avenue, Milwaukee, WI 53218 2 oz, $2.69	X	X	✔	✔	X	✔	✔	✔	✔	X	X	✔	✔	✔

✔ Works with no problems   — Has little or no effect   X Not recommended

model before the decal is positioned, Fig. 3. Many setting solutions contain wetting agents that help prevent tiny air bubbles from getting trapped underneath the decal.

Now, soak a single decal in lukewarm water for a few seconds. Don't try to get too far ahead — work with one piece at a time. Too many pieces soaking may leave you with lots of tiny decals floating in your water dish, and they're hard to catch and keep flat. Set the wet decal aside for one minute or until it moves freely on the paper. Using tweezers, carefully position the decal (still on the paper) over the proper location on the model, Fig. 4. Slide the decal off the paper by holding the decal in place with a cotton swab, paintbrush, or soft eraser and pulling the

backing paper away. This method is especially helpful with long, thin decals.

Once the decal is in position, apply more setting solution, making sure the entire decal is wet, Fig. 5. Don't touch the decal after the solution is applied — it's getting soft and starting to snuggle down onto the painted surface of the model. If you try to move it, the extra-soft decal may tear. Touch a dry cotton swab to the edge of the decal to remove excess setting solution. As the decal-setting solution works, it may wrinkle and distort the decal. This is normal and *usually* harmless — the decal should flatten out as it dries. If it doesn't, then your setting solution isn't compatible with that brand of decal (see Fig. 8). Move along one side of the model, applying one decal at a time,

then put the model aside to dry for a few hours before starting the other side.

After all the decals are dry, soak a cotton swab in water and mop up stains from water and setting solution that may have pooled in corners and recesses in the model's surface, Fig. 6. It important to clean up these stains some decal adhesives, setting solutions, and waterborne minerals may discolor the model later on.

Check all the decals carefully. Are there bubbles or areas that need more setting solution? If so, apply more and repeat the procedure. Let the model dry at least 24 hours before applying any overcoats.

The last step is to apply a clear overcoat. This seals the decal and provides a consistent finish to the model. The

CUSTOM-MADE DECALS

It's possible to have decals custom made. You can do it yourself with blank decal paper and a copier (see "Making your own decals," November/December 1985 FSM), but this has limitations. You can have a decal company print them, but it isn't cheap, so keep that in mind when you plan your sheet. Each color adds to the price. Most companies require camera-ready artwork twice the size of the final decal, black image on white paper. Contact the company for specifics on sizes, colors, quantities, and prices.

We asked the companies below to indicate their prices, minimum orders, and completion times to produce a 4-color, 3" x 5" decal (customer provides artwork) for 10, 100, 500, and 1,000 copies. The information they provided is included.

- Jeff's Decals, 1747 Selby Avenue, St. Paul, MN 55104: 10 copies, $96.00; 100, $446.00; 500, $1,956.00; 1,000, $3,656.00; 2 weeks
- Donald B. Manlick, 2127 South 11th Street, Manitowoc, WI 54220: 25 copies (minimum), $255.45; 100, $549.90; 500, $1,755.78; 7 weeks
- Rail Graphics, 1111 Beechwood Road, Buffalo Grove, IL 60090: 25 copies (minimum), $180.00; 100, $360.00; 500, $1,584.00; 1,000, $2,574.00; 4 weeks
- Screen Print Unlimited, Suite 308, 3417 Roger B. Chaffee Memorial Boulevard, Grand Rapids, MI 49508: 500 (minimum), $655.00; 1,000, $1,070.00; 3 weeks
- Woodland Scenics (dry transfers), P. O. Box 98, Linn Creek, MO 65052: 200 copies (minimum), $518.00; 500, $1,295.00; 1,000, $2,590.00; 5 weeks

ecal is sandwiched between two coats f clear paint and protects the decal om humidity, dust, and dirt. Microcale's so-called "Micro System" is essentially this process, but it can be one with almost any brands of decals, etting solutions, and clear coats.

Some modelers apply an additional loss coat over the decals even when ne final finish is flat. This evens out ne surface and hides the clear film. If ou apply this gloss coat, wait another 4 hours before applying a final flat oat. In either case, dust on a light coat rst. Flooding on an overcoat may arm the decals and paint.

Decal-setting solutions. There are any decal-setting solutions on the arket. Which is best? Well, a solution nat is best for a certain brand of decal an destroy another brand. Your best et is to test a setting solution on an nimportant decal piece to determine

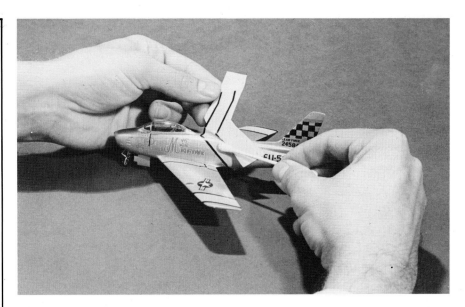

Fig. 4. A cotton swab is used to hold the decal in place as the backing paper is slipped out from underneath.

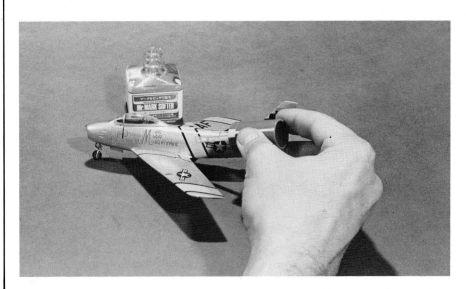

Fig. 5. More setting solution is applied over the decal. After this, don't touch the decal — it's soft and easily damaged.

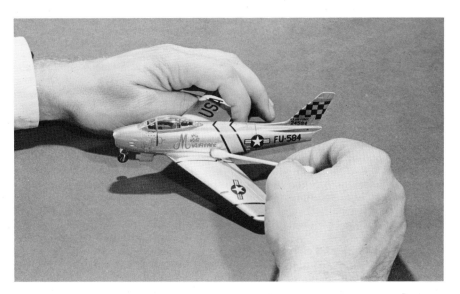

Fig. 6. Wipe off water and setting solution stains before applying a clear overcoat.

Decals 101

SOLVING DECAL PROBLEMS

Here are the common decal problems and ways to prevent or correct them.

● **Silvering.** The clear areas of the decals have a shiny, silver appearance under certain lighting conditions. This happens when the decal is not in contact with the surface of the paint. Flat paints cause the decal to "float" on the rough surface, allowing air underneath. Light traveling through both the clear film and the air trapped underneath causes the silvering effect. Use gloss paints or a clear gloss coat over flat paints. A decal-setting solution will help, too.

Clear film silvers over flat paint

NO STEP

● **Decal is melting.** The decal is distorted and torn, probably caused by a concentration of setting solution or one that is too strong for the decal. Dilute the solution or try another brand.

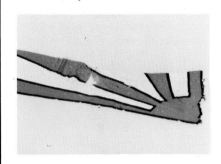

Stains

● **Stains.** Dry white or reddish-brown blotches, often in corners of the model and around the decals, are caused by accumulations of decal adhesives, setting solutions, and waterborne minerals. Be sure to absorb excess water and setting solutions before they dry. Wipe the area with a damp cloth or cotton swab before applying the clear overcoat.

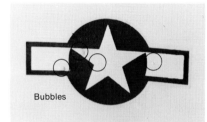

Bubbles

● **Bubbles.** Tiny air bubbles are trapped under the decal. Prick them with a sharp pin or knife blade and apply more setting solution.

● **Tangled decal.** You moved the decal too much and it has folded over itself and hopelessly snarled. Remove the decal from the model and float it in water, where it will straighten out. Place the decal on the original paper or waxed paper and reapply (carefully) to the model.

● **Yellow clear carrier film.** Clear areas of the decal that have a yellow tinge are caused by acids in the backing paper, usually found on old decal sheets. Tape the decal face out on a south-facing window. After several weeks or months, sunlight will bleach out the yellow film. Inspect the decal periodically; sunlight could also bleach out red and yellow pigments on the decal, but this should not occur before the clear film bleaches out. Make sure the window

doesn't "sweat" from indoor humidity. If the decal gets wet and is allowed to dry, it may not come off the decal paper again.

● **Fractures.** The decal disintegrates as it soaks in the water. This is caused by a clear carrier film that is too thin or one that has been adversely affected by temperature and humidity. If this is a new sheet, take it back to your dealer for replacement. Microscale's Micro Super Film or a clear coat applied over the decal sheet will act as a carrier film, but each piece will have to be cut out individually. Always store decals in a cool, dry environment.

● **Ink runs.** The colors begin to run and stain the model. Oops! Your setting solution is dissolving the inks. Try another brand or don't use any setting solution at all. This problem may occur with foreign-made and offset-printed decals.

● **Decal doesn't stick or respond to setting solution.** No matter how much setting solution you pile on the decal, it remains stiff and doesn't conform to the surface detail. Some older decals were printed with carriers and inks that are not affected by your setting solution. Experiment with other solutions. If none works, dilute white glue in water, brush it onto the model, and apply the decals. This will help attach the decal but won't make it conform.

---

its effect. Of course, this could mean buying many setting solutions and testing them before you find one that works best. To save you time and trouble, I gathered 9 decal-setting solutions and tested them on 14 brands of decals, Fig. 7.

Since I was interested only in the effect of the solutions on the decals, I applied nine markings of each decal brand listed in the table to a sheet of unpainted Evergreen sheet styrene

grooved to simulate metal siding (page 47). The grooves test the solution's ability to soften the decal so that it conforms to the uneven surface.

I applied each decal-setting solution to the decals, let them dry, doused them again, and observed the effects. Figure 8 shows the results. A check mark means that the solution worked on that brand of decal without any problems. A hyphen means that the solution had little or no effect on that

brand of decal. An X means that the solution had an undesirable effect on the decal (dissolved decal, ran the inks, or otherwise destroyed the decal).

The stronger setting solutions made the inks run on the British Airfix and Modeldecal brands, and the offset-printed AMT/Ertl and Monogram, Fig. 9. Some of the thicker decals did not respond to some setting solutions, while some of the thinner ones did well with all solutions. Although I had no prob

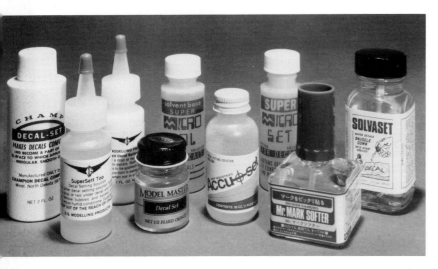

g. 7. Commercial decal-setting solutions come in a variety of formulas and strengths

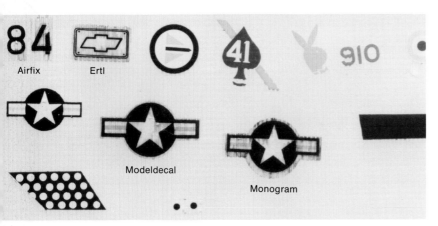

Airfix Ertl

Modeldecal

Monogram

g. 9. The inks contained in Airfix, Ertl, Modeldecal, and Monogram decals ran when ronger setting solutions were used.

ms in my tests, I have had experinces where Solvaset caused Microale decals to shrivel up.

Super Scale International and Scale-Iaster produce decals for Testor's kits. artograph makes decals for Italeri,

ESCI, and some aftermarket auto and aircraft decal sets.

There's no guarantee that my results will hold true in every case. Kit manufacturers usually stick with one printer for their decals, but they may change

printers or printing methods. A solution that worked on the decals I tested might destroy older or newer sets. It's still a good idea to test your solution on a small, unimportant decal before you risk the whole sheet.   **FSM**

SOURCES

Here are the addresses of aftermarket decal companies. Look for their products at your local hobby shop.

- Americals, 4373 Varsity Lane, Houston, TX 77004: 1/72 and 1/48 WWI aircraft
- ATP, 3014 Abelia Court, San Jose, CA 95121: 1/200 and 1/144 airliners
- Autodecal, Auto World International, 701 N. Keyser Ave., Scranton, PA 18508: automobiles
- Fred Cady Design, P. O. Box 576, Mount Prospect, IL 60056: 1/24, 1/25, 1/43 automobiles
- Experts-Choice Decals, Bare-Metal Foil Company, P. O. Box 82, Farmington, MI 48024: 1/72 and 1/48 military aircraft
- Detail & Scale Decals, P. O. Box 2190, Peachtree City, GA 30269: 1/32, 1/48, 1/72 military aircraft
- E. S. Scale Models, 1649 Fairfield Court, No. 1, Ontario, CA 91761: fire apparatus
- Gold Medal Models, 12332 Chapman Ave., No. 81, Garden Grove, CA 92640: 1/350 and 1/700 ships
- Super Scale International, 2211 Mouton Drive, Carson City, NV 89706: 1/32, 1/48, 1/72, 1/144 aircraft
- Midcontinent Miniatures, 303 Woodson Drive, Raymore, MO 64083: trucks
- Modeldecal, Modeltoys, 246 Kingston Road, Portsmouth, Hants. PO2 7LR, England: 1/72 military aircraft
- Scale-Master, Aeolus Publishing Ltd., 512-115 W. California Ave., Vista, CA 92083: 1/144, 1/72, 1/48 aircraft

Sources

A+B Epoxy Putty: see Putty

Adhesives
  IPS Weld-On #3 and #4: Industrial Polychemical Service, P.O. Box 471, Gardena, CA 90247
  Micro Weld: Microscale Industries, P.O. Box 11950, Costa Mesa, CA 92627
  Tenax 7R: Hebco Enterprises, Spencerport, NY 14559
Ammunition and ration boxes: Verlinden Products, VLS Mail Order, Lone Star Industrial Park, O'Fallon, MO 63366
Aircraft templates: Verlinden Products (address above)

B

Bolt heads: Grandt Line Products Inc., 1040B Shary Court, Concord, CA 94518
Brass parts
  Cal-Scale, P.O. Box 322, Montoursville, PA 17754
  K&S Engineering, 6917 West 59th St., Chicago, IL 60638
  LMG Enterprises, 1627 S. 26th St., Sheboygan, WI 53081

C

Celluclay: Activa Products Inc., Marshall, TX 75670
Chain
  Campbell Scale Models, c/o Wm. K. Walthers Inc., P. O. Box 18676, Milwaukee, WI 53218
  Clover House, Box 62D, Sebastopol, CA 95473
Contrail rod and tubing: Imported Specialties, 3655 Sullivant Ave., Columbus, OH 43228

D

Decals
  Americals, 4373 Varsity Lane, Houston, TX 77004
  ATP/Airliners America, 3014 Abelia Court, San Jose, CA 95121
  Autodecal, Auto World International, 701 N. Keyser Ave., Scranton, PA 18508
  Bare-Metal Foil & Hobby Co., P. O. Box 82, Farmington, MI 48024
  Detail & Scale, P.O. Box 2190, Peachtree City, GA 30269
  E. S. Scale Models, 1649 Fairfield Court No. 1, Ontario, CA 91761
  Fred Cady Design, P.O. Box 576, Mount Prospect, IL 60056
  California Decals, P. O. Box 7101, Oakland, CA 94601
  Gold Medal Models, 12332 Chapman Ave., No. 81, Garden Grove, CA 92640
  Midcontinent Miniatures, 303 Woodson Drive, Raymore, MO 64083
  Modeldecal, Modeltoys, 246 Kingston Road, Portsmouth, Hants, PO2 7LR, England

Scale-Master, Aeolus Publishing, 512-115 W. California Ave., Vista, CA 92083
Super Scale International, 2211 Mouton, Carson City, NV 89706
Diesel locomotive data sheet: Microscale Industries, P.O. Box 11950, Costa Mesa, CA 92627
Dremel Moto-Tool: Emerson Electric Co., P.O. Box 1468, Racine, WI 53401
Dry transfers: Chartpak/Pickett, 1 River Road, Leeds, MA 01053
Duratite: see Putty

F

Filler putty: see Putty
Flex-I-File: Creations Unlimited, 2939 Montreat Drive N.E., Grand Rapids, MI 49505
Foil: Bare-Metal Foil & Hobby Co., P. O. Box 82, Farmington, MI 48024
Formaline: see Tape
Fotocut: see Photoetched parts

G

Glue: see Adhesives

H

Hood and trunk pins, photoetched: see Photoetched parts
Hot Tool: 7 Hawkes St., P. O. Box 615, Marblehead, MA 01945

I

IPS Weld-On: see Adhesives

L

Lead foil: VLS Mail Order, Lone Star Industrial Park, O'Fallon, MO 63366
License plates: Tyresmoke Industries, available from Model Storehouse, 8580 Gaines Ave., Orangevale, CA 95662
License-plate decals: see Decals
License-plate frames: Detail Master, P. O. Box 1465, Sterling, VA 22170
Lumber, scale
  Kappler Mill & Lumber Co., 1760 Monrovia, A-15, Costa Mesa, CA 92627
  Northeastern Scale Models, 99 Cross St., P.O. Box 727, Methuen, MA 01844

M

Metalizer: see Paint
Micro Weld: see Adhesives

P

Paint, metallic
  Metalizer, Testor Corp., 620 Buckbee St., Rockford, IL 61108
  SnJ Spray Metal: SnJ Model Products, P. O. Box 28024, Sacramento, CA 95828
Photo resist and chemicals
  Datak Corp., North Bergen, NJ 07047

GC Electronics, Hydrometals Inc., Rockford, IL 61101
Photoetched parts
  Detail Master, P. O. Box 1465, Sterling, VA 22170
  The Floating Drydock, c/o General Delivery, Kresgeville, PA 18333
  Fotocut, Erieville Rd., Box 120, Erieville, NY 13061
  Gold Medal Models, 12332 Chapman Ave., No. 81, Garden Grove, CA 92640
  IPMS/USA, P.O. Box 6369, Lincoln, NE 68506
  Model Technologies, 13472 5th St., Suite 12, Chino, CA 91710
  S & S Specialties, P. O. Box 222, Bedford, TX 76095
  Tom's Modelworks, 1050 Cranberry Dr., Cupertino, CA 95014
  Tripart, available from Marco Polo Import, 532 S. Coralridge Place, Industry, CA 91746
  Unique Scale Hobbies, 1178 Boston Road, Springfield, MA 01119
  Verlinden Products: VLS Mail Order, Lone Star Industrial Park, O'Fallon, MO 63366
  Waldron Model Products, P.O. Box 431, Merlin, OR 97532
Plastruct: see Styrene building materials
Punch-and-die set: Waldron Model Products, P.O. Box 431, Merlin, OR 97532
Putty
  A+B Epoxy Putty: The Biggs Co., 612 E. Franklin, El Segundo, CA 90245
  Duratite: DAP Inc., Dayton, OH 45401

S

SnJ Model Products: see Paint
Screen, brass: LMG Enterprises, 1627 S. 26th St., Sheboygan, WI 5308
Screen, plastic: Clover House, Box 62D, Sebastopol, CA 95473
Seat-belt buckles, photoetched: see Photoetched parts
Stencils, tire: Replicas and Miniatures of Maryland, 7479-D Furnace Branch Road, Glen Burnie, MD 21061
Styrene building materials
  Evergreen Scale Models, 12808 N. E. 125th Way, Kirkland, WA 98034
  Plastruct, 1020 S. Wallace Place, City of Industry, CA 91748

T

Tape, graphic
  Chartpak/Pickett, 1 River Road, Leeds, MA 01053
  Formaline: Graphic Products Corp., 3601 Edison Place, Rolling Meadows, IL 60008
Tenax 7R: see Adhesives

W

Wire, floral: Western Trimming Corp., Chatsworth, CA 91311